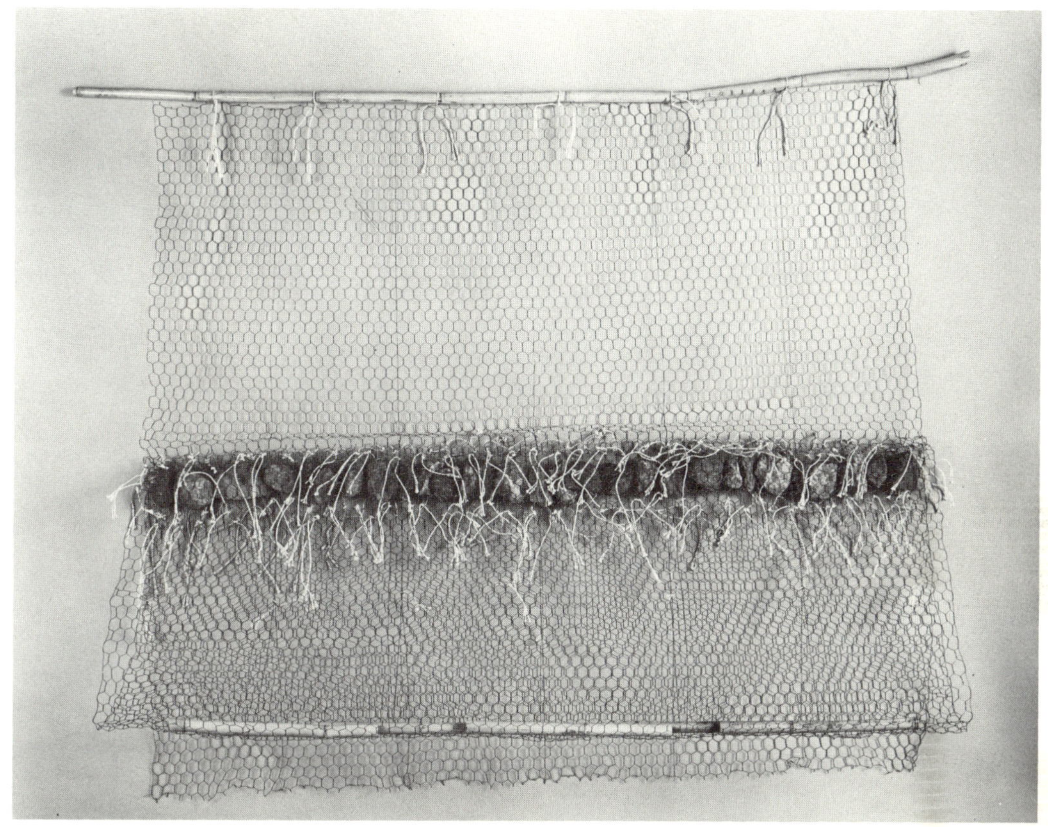

Stut/Struss, 1972
chicken wire, rocks,
string, bamboo
38″ x 5′9″ x 21″
Collection Los
Angeles County
Museum of Art,
Contemporary Art
Council, New Talent
and Purchase Award

Jud Fine

Ronald J. Onorato

La Jolla Museum of Contemporary Art
August 19 – October 2, 1988

de Saisset Museum, Santa Clara University
January 21 – March 12, 1989

Initiated and sponsored by the Fellows of Contemporary Art, Los Angeles, and supported
in part by a grant from the National Endowment for the Arts, a federal agency.

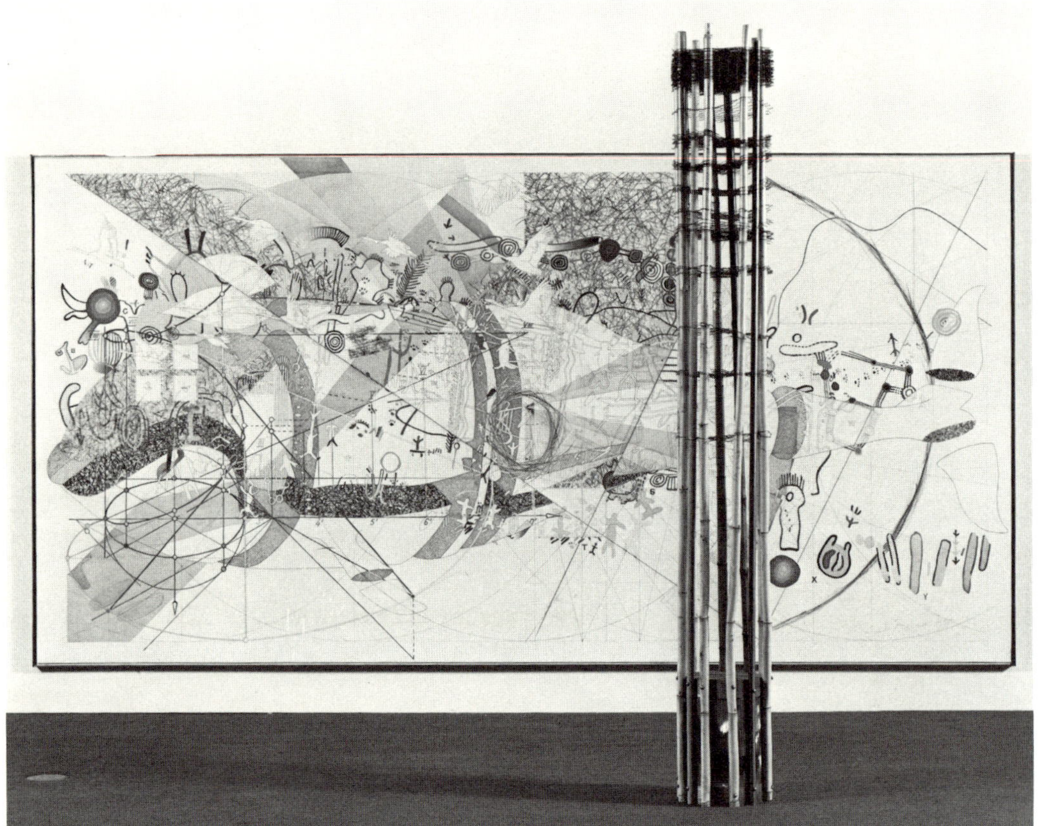

Dbl. OR, 1985
oilstick, oil paint,
acrylic, graphite,
ink, colored ink,
prisma stick,
bamboo, chicken
wire, steel, stainless
steel, wood, canvas
6'10" x 13', column
8' x 12" diameter
Collection Santa
Barbara Museum of
Art: Gift of Barry and
Gail Berkus

*We dedicate this exhibition and catalogue to the memory of Susan B. Kockritz and
Lois P. Osborn, two true pillars of the La Jolla Museum of Contemporary Art and
loyal supporters of the arts in Southern California. Their energizing presence and
great good humor are sorely missed, but their generous spirits and high standards
continue to inspire us all.*

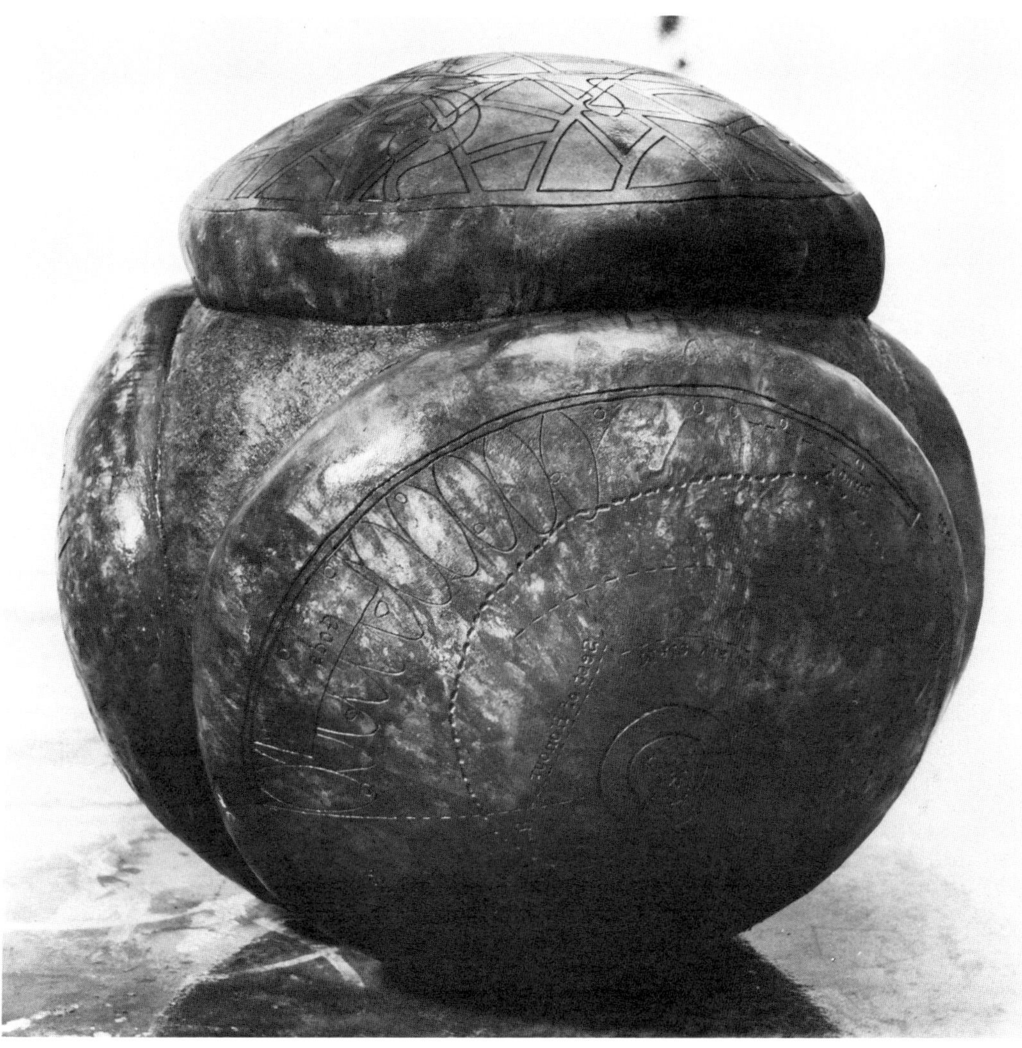

Contents

Foreword

The Fellows of Contemporary Art are honored to initiate and sponsor the exhibition **Jud Fine** at the La Jolla Museum of Contemporary Art. This, an exhibition of versatile media including sculpture, painting and drawing, affords a unique opportunity for the Fellows, as sponsors, to continue their support of those artists who constitute the contemporary art world of Southern California.
Jud Fine is the fifteenth exhibition sponsored by the Fellows in the thirteen years since its formation. Exhibits have been mounted in a wide variety of exhibition spaces including the Frederick S. Wight Art Gallery at the University of California, Los Angeles; the Los Angeles Institute of Contemporary Art (LAICA); the Otis Art Institute Gallery, Los Angeles; the Newport Harbor Art Museum; the San Francisco Museum of Modern Art; the Laguna Art Museum; the Gallery at the Plaza, Security Pacific National Bank, Los Angeles; the Los Angeles Municipal Art Gallery; the Fisher Gallery at the University of Southern California; the Museum of Contemporary Art, Los Angeles; LACE (Los Angeles Contemporary Exhibitions); and the Santa Barbara Museum of Art. The initiation of fifteen exhibitions at such varied and prestigious venues confirms the Fellows' continuing support of and contribution to the arena of contemporary art.

The Fellows wish to thank a number of individuals who were instrumental in both the planning and execution of the **Jud Fine** exhibition. First, our thanks to Hugh M. Davies, Director of the La Jolla Museum of Contemporary Art, for his unfailing graciousness and constant assistance to the project and for his unflagging support of the Fellows over the past several years. Our thanks, also, to Ronald J. Onorato, Senior Curator and essayist for the catalogue. His exceptional talents were applied to all aspects of the exhibition, and its aesthetic excellence is due to his efforts.

Further, special thanks to Madeleine Grynsztejn, Associate Curator, who so skillfully coordinated the myriad details attendant to the exhibition, and to Toby Smith for her good advice and generally good offices relative to the exhibition. Thanks also to Joan and Charles Cochrane, gracious and diligent liaisons between the Fellows and the La Jolla Museum of Contemporary Art.

Finally, with great appreciation, we acknowledge the superior efforts of Murray (Mickey) Gribin, whose traits of unflappability and innate perceptiveness molded the entire exhibition into a viable entity.

George N. Epstein, Chairman
Fellows of Contemporary Art

Introduction

One of the first opportunities upon my arrival in La Jolla five years ago was the invitation to propose an exhibition for sponsorship by the Fellows of Contemporary Art. Following consultation with the curators and explanation of the Fellows' mandate, we were delighted to be given the privilege of preparing the current survey exhibition of Jud Fine's work. Jud Fine is that all too rare native son who has achieved great success in the world of art and ideas yet has remained an Angelino for more than forty years. He has drawn support and stimulation from this region both as an artist and a teacher and he has given back more. This exhibition is a celebration of a mutually enriching and ongoing relationship between artist and audience.

Growing up with a surname loaded toward excellence seems appropriate for Jud. His work from the earliest poles to the most recent paintings/sculptures has consistently been intellectually and visually ambitious. He has always cultivated complexity and depth against the grain of a culture which craves the fast in food and thought. A clever and curious artist/philosopher, he layers his work with ever richer content and meaning to engage and reward the viewer/fellow traveler no matter how shallow or deep his or her engagement may be.

Ron Onorato is a scholar and curator who delights in a meaty dialogue. The evidence of his informative introductory essay—both its form and content devised to elucidate Fine—attests to the stimulating meeting of these two sympathetic minds. We are all enormously grateful to Jud and to Ron for this fine exhibition and catalogue. We are likewise indebted to the Fellows of Contemporary Art and the National Endowment for the Arts for their generous subvention of the project.

Hugh M. Davies
Director

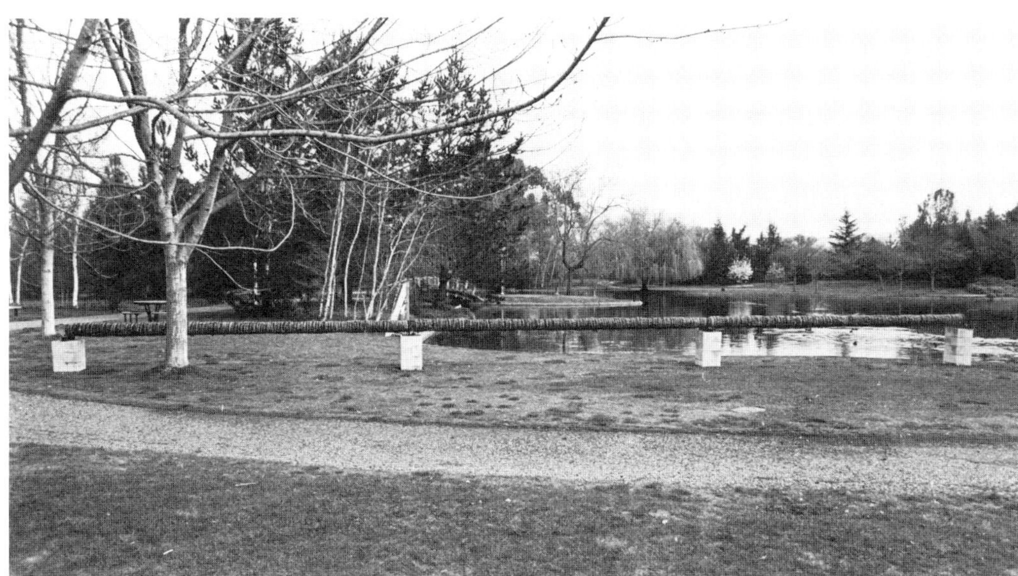

Horizontal Pillar
#3, 1982
steel, applewood,
straw, string, wire
60′ x 8½″ diameter
Site work, California
State University,
Sonoma

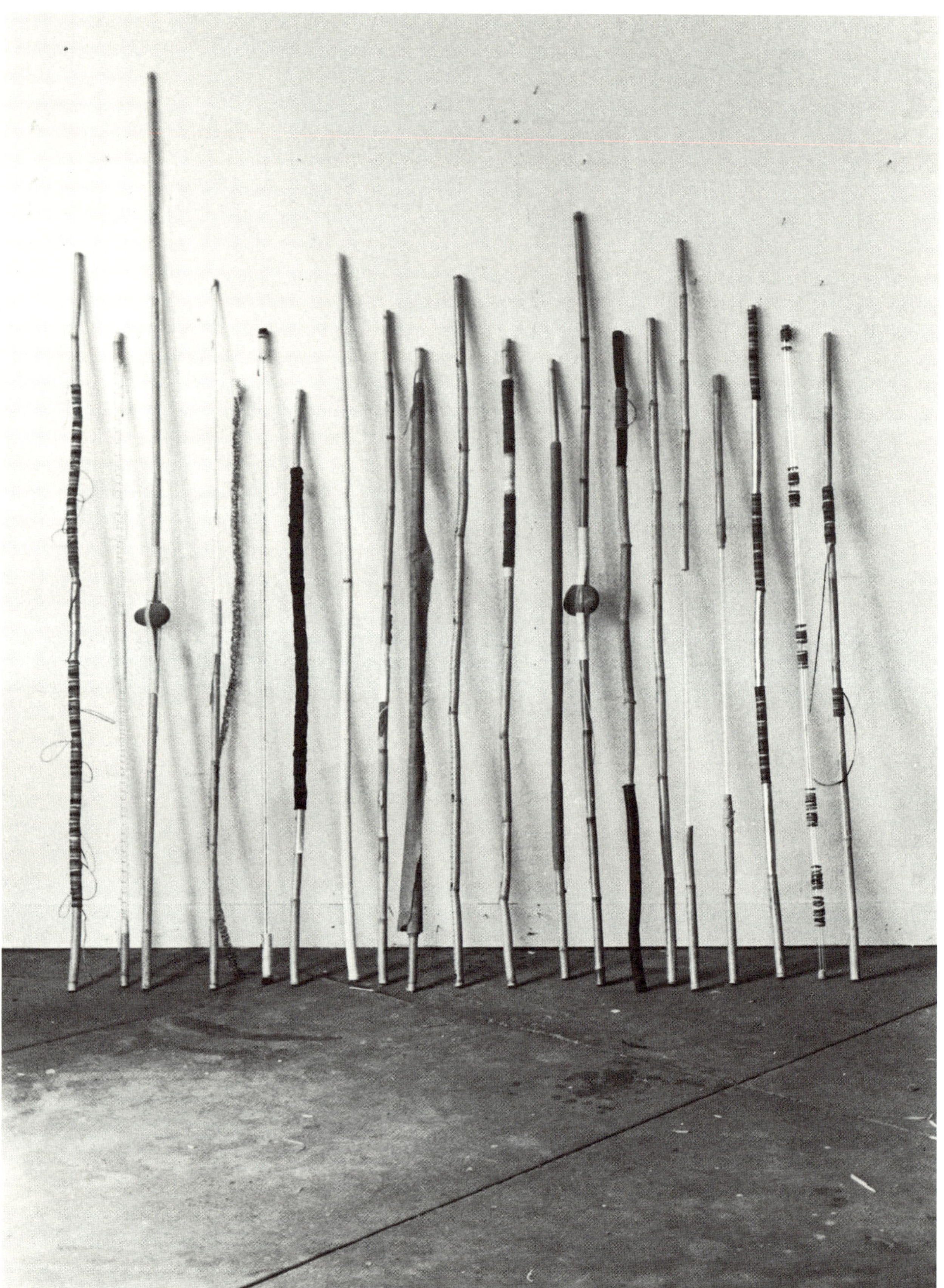

Telling Acts: The Art of Jud Fine

Ronald J. Onorato

. . . you prefer it this way, confronting something and not quite
knowing yet what it is.   Italo Calvino[1]

A compilation of the continuum that was or appears to have been Red Green.[*]

Jud Fine's art has always been about communicating, or more precisely, about both the possibilities and impossibilities of communicating. Employing a wealth of message systems—texts, graphic and numerical symbols, visual, mythological, and scientific vocabularies—Fine has explored both the stories he tells and their telling, his subjects and their narration. To accomplish this, Fine has never winnowed his means to one, particular mode but has instead utilized performance, writing, graphic design, object and environmental sculpture, and painting to manifest his ideas about language in its broadest sense. Such a multiplicity of means and devices has predictably left Fine without a clearly defined niche, as critics and writers have been unable to discern that which is consistently at the core of all his work—the act of telling.

Born in 1944 of Irish father and Mexican mother. Father—in Mexico—vague—intertwined somehow with Mexican Nazi sympathies, Irish neutrality and the IRA—he wanted his son to be a citizen of the world. Mother—daughter in upwardly mobile Mexican middle class family—both scandalized by the liaison and later pleased because the couple married—but moved to the international community of San Miguel Allende.

Narration is, after all, among the most primal of human activities. It is, in its broadest sense, how all communication takes place as we put observations, opinions, desires, and experiences into a particular sequence with linguistic or visual metaphors encompassing time and space. All human activity contains aspects of narration—magic and science describe the physical world around us in processional terms, religion and myths convey our hopes and fears about birth and death, passing norms of cultural behavior and values from one generation to the next, and even the crafts retell the process of their making. In popular language the connection between a physical, handworked craft and storytelling is made often as we speak of spinning a yarn, weaving a tale, character sketches, word painters, and pen craft.

◄ *The Arab and his Friends,* 1970
bamboo, steel, mixed media
overall dimension
9′ x 12′
Collection Dr. Herbert Burda, West Germany

[1] Italo Calvino, *If on a Winter's Night a Traveler,* William Weaver, trans. (San Diego: Harcourt Brace Jovanovich, 1981), 9.

[*] Jud Fine, "Rojo 'Red' Green (1944–1984): A Work of Intent Discovered with Analysis." Unpublished text, 1974. All subsequent entries reproduce without editing this complete text.

History recounts a selective ordering of previous events, while literature and art (at least in today's idioms) are capable of recapitulating both past and future contexts within the physical— optic and haptic—perceptions of the present.

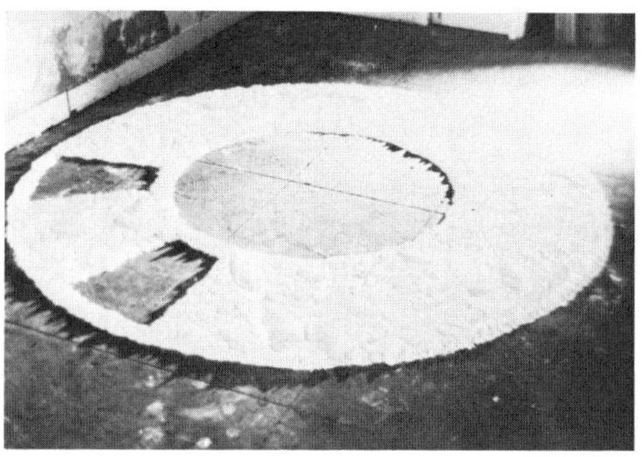

Anthro Ring, 1970
(destroyed)
body prints in dry
plaster
20′ diameter
site work, artist's
studio, Venice,
California

Even a cursory survey of Fine's art work reveals an involvement with all these cultural activities; his densely layered imagery, interwoven on canvas or paper, in objects or environments, is a static cacophony of information being broadcast and received from myriad sources. It is as if Fine intuitively senses the inherently eclectic panoramic potential of his chosen metier, for, as Roland Barthes succinctly stated, narrative "is simply there like life itself . . . international, transhistorical, transcultural."[2]

Fine's earliest mature works from around 1970, which partake of a performance-conceptual-installation idiom, all read as visual documentation of a series of events. That is, they represent for his viewers some sequence of activity, recounting its original presence: whether it is the artist moving across a hearth-like ring of powder (*Anthro Ring,* 1970), his surveying a period of his own work (*Los Angeles 1970,* 1973)[3], or evoking an aboriginal site of great spatial, ritual, and narrative power (*Ayers' Analog,* 1974). With each piece he continually records the physical process of its making—be it his bodily movements, his passage through a place or the universal effects of gravity, inertia, material strengths, and balances (*Stut/Struss,* 1972).

---

[2]Roland Barthes, "Introduction to the Structural Analysis of Narratives," *Images, Music, Text,* Stephen Heath, trans. New York, 1977, p. 79 as quoted in *On Narrative,* W. J. T. Mitchell, ed. (Chicago: The University of Chicago Press, 1980, 1981).

[3]Fine has intentionally created pictorial or text works that self-reflexively recapitulate journal-like a period of his career or his thinking: *Los Angeles, 1970,* 1973, *Confessions,* 1976, *Annotation,* 1986–87, etc.

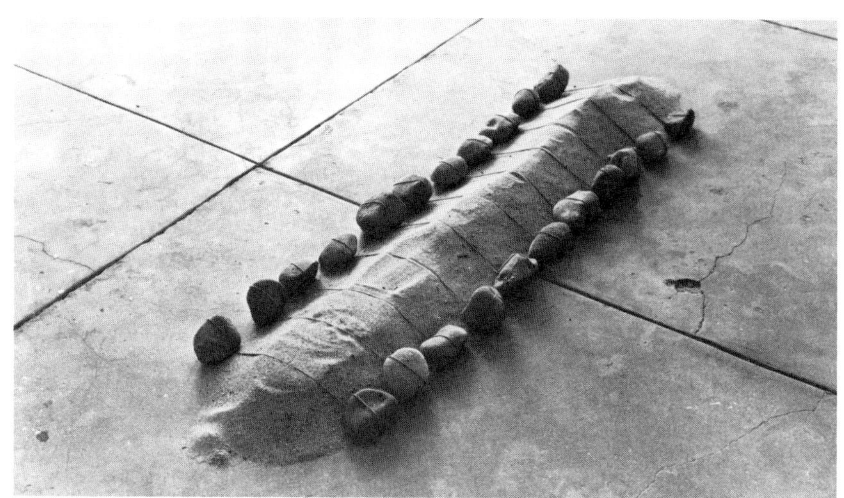

► *Untitled* (destroyed), 1970 sand, rock, string, acrylic 8′ x 24″ site work, artist's studio, Venice, California

▼ *Untitled* (destroyed), 1970 sand, rock, string, acrylic 8′ x 24″ site work, Santa Monica Mountains, California

While others have detailed Fine's emergence from the then current context of sculpture making and its concerns for seriality, physical properties and spatial environment, a fuller reading of Fine's art reveals a different set of art parallels.[1] While his initial forays during the late 1960s were inevitably informed by the hegemony of minimalist concerns, with his subsequent move back to California after graduate school in the east, his interests seem more in concert with the nascent Angeleno art tendency toward literary concerns. Rather than the industrial fabrications of a Richard Serra or a Michael Heizer, a framework of storytelling formulated by Ed Ruscha, John Baldessari, or Roland Reiss was influencing young Southern California artists and has been developed subsequently by a diverse group of artists on both coasts, including Allen Ruppersberg, Alexis Smith, Alice Aycock, Vernon Fisher, and Fine.

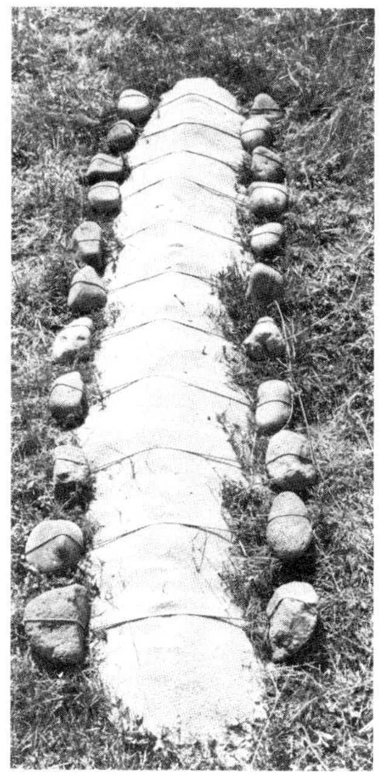

Red/Green continuum: R. Green is vague. He is well documented in a minor travel journal (cr. 1973) from a passage written in Amsterdam—captured by an artistic imagination his existence henceforth became a sublimation of the general tendencies of the time. "A vision that seemed to be unique in its externally undefined and internally unself-defined singularity." It went straight and it was somewhere, but where? This singularity of purpose, in total, added up to something, but what? R. Green is dead. So he is history. An analysis can therefore be objectivified—bias can be cataloged cleanly in perception of the object. Idea of a life as a round whole—a circular, linear, additive continuum. Why and how did R. Green die? Why was he then a subject of a mortuary cannibalism? What was it about him that pre-ordained and approved that

[1]The best overview of Fine's work is Robert L. Pincus, "Vision, Concept and Object: The Art of Jud Fine, 1970–1985," *Jud Fine*, exhibition catalogue (Los Angeles: Los Angeles Municipal Gallery, 1985), 7–16, although I disagree that language is for Fine a "gloss on the visual and physical aspects of the work."

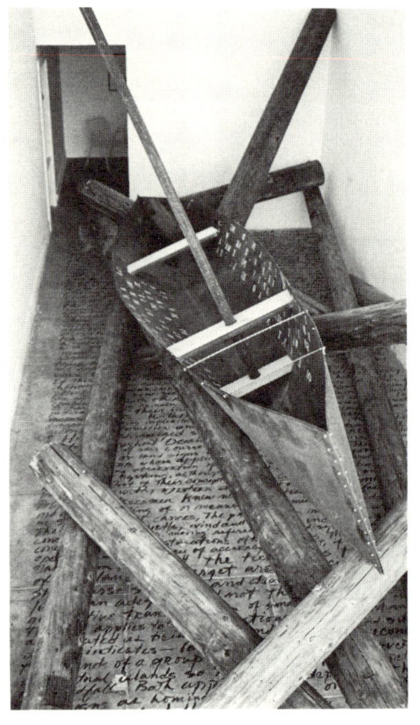

*A Physical
Narration without
Plot*, 1985
wood, steel, enamel
16′ x 14′ x 36″
installation,
Installation Gallery,
San Diego,
California

Fine's stylistic "primitivism" links his work to the widely disparate
range of artists in the seventies, from Aycock and Robert Morris to
Michelle Stuart, Alan Shields and Robert Stackhouse, who investi-
gated the forms, rituals, and myths of prehistoric cultures. If there
is another artistic ancestry in Fine's work, it would likely be trace-
able through Robert Smithson to Marcel Duchamp, both of whose
pseudo-scientific musings and involvement with arcana were
often a diffuse means to a very elegant end. Engaging social and
anthropological concerns, like the act of storytelling itself, Fine's
art is not readily linked to a single, clarifying source but remains
tangential to a world of influences and motivations—some within
and many from outside the world of art.

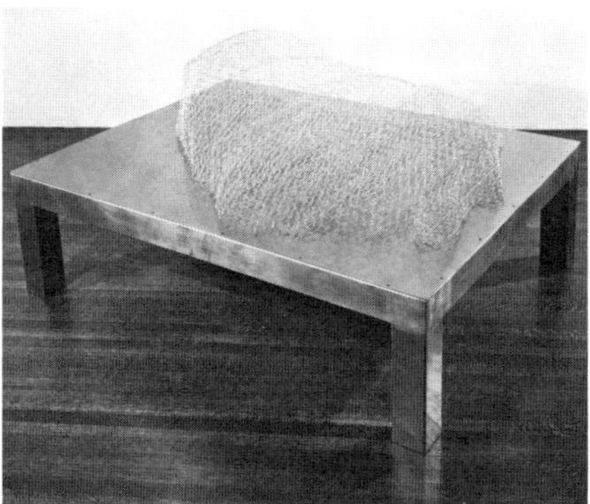

Ayers' Analog, 1974
steel, chicken wire,
acid etched steel
36″ x 60″ x 48″
Collection Power
Institute of Fine Arts,
University of Sydney,
Sydney, Australia

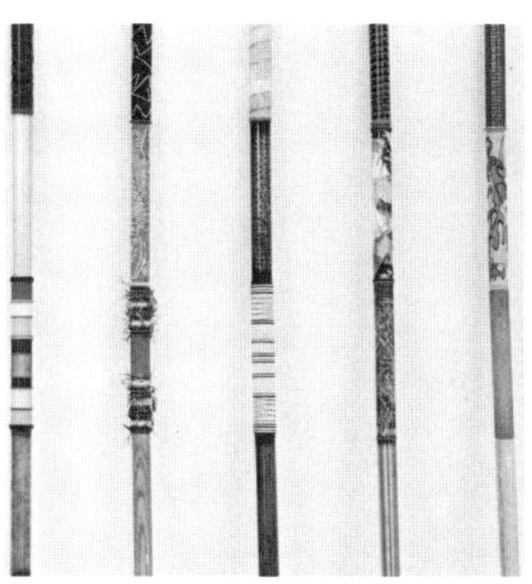

Poles from *Watt/ Analogy* series,
1981–1987 (detail)
mixed media on
bamboo, steel,
stainless steel
Each pole 8′9″ x 2″
diameter
Courtesy Ronald
Feldman Fine Arts,
New York City

In Fine's best known art works, his ongoing series of poles initiated in the the early seventies, his viewers are presented with a primary form—tall, thin verticals so inherently simple that they depend on the surrounding architecture for support. Rather than suggesting the kind of serialized formats of found materials or the mute sentinels of the minimalist aesthetic, these read more like recording objects, or better yet, artifacts, where texts, colors, ornamentation, and patterns combine across a single coherent skin.

Red was neither dumb nor smart—yet his intelligence appears

to have been acute, perhaps because he threw out so much, its

singularity reads as a clarity.

When they are set in a row against a wall, the handwrought detailing of each vertical combines with its neighbors into a broad, slanted rectangle where themes of color, striation, and surface are interwoven as if on a traditional canvas (remember the textile idioms of weaving a tale?). An appropriate literary analogy might equate pole with paragraph, grouping to chapter.

Another key early work, *Ayers' Analog*, 1974, reiterates Fine's literary concerns but posits them in broader cultural, social history terms. *Ayers' Analog* is a sculpture combining a wire form in the shape of the famous geological formation in central Australia surmounting a table/base whose top is etched with a self-reflexive text which may be at least partly read through the open lattice work of the chicken wire "rock" form. In his own meta-critical fashion, Fine's text is both a part of the art work and its most succinct commentary:

Ayers Rock is at once secular and religious. It dominates a culture that has no conception of history, no succession of events, no past or future. The rock has remained unchanged and unchanging since it erupted from a flat, sandy, featureless plain simultaneously with the emergence of the Pitjandjara aborigines that inhabit its surroundings. It contains the essence of psychic and physical survival. Every nuance of Pitjandjara's mythic and worldly life has some counterpart in the physical features of the rock. The rock therefore owes its sense, meaning and purpose to a social elaboration. It is the Pitjandjara's self-invested connection with themselves.[5]

Recent critics have failed to elucidate Fine's art, calling it everything from engagingly direct to cold and intellectual, casual and off-handed, on the cusp and arty to radically infracritical[6] Taking a cue from Fine's own interest, we might more productively borrow critical terms from literary analysis to deconstruct Fine's art.

In *Ayers' Analog*, the recent monumental painting *Annotation*, 1986-87, and his sculpture *Neo*, 1987-88, Fine reveals three levels of experience which motivate communication: first, visual experience, which tends toward the descriptive (or possibly ornamental) text; secondly, the anthropological or broadly cultural experience which, when layered onto visual data includes language, symbols, and meaning. This second realm of experience motivates narration. Finally, there is speculative experience concerning the relationship between self and the world, the dimensions of the mind. From description and narration we move into the arena of meditation. These experiences and their results might be recast temporally as the visual equated with present experience, the narrative with past experience, and the speculative with future projection.[7]

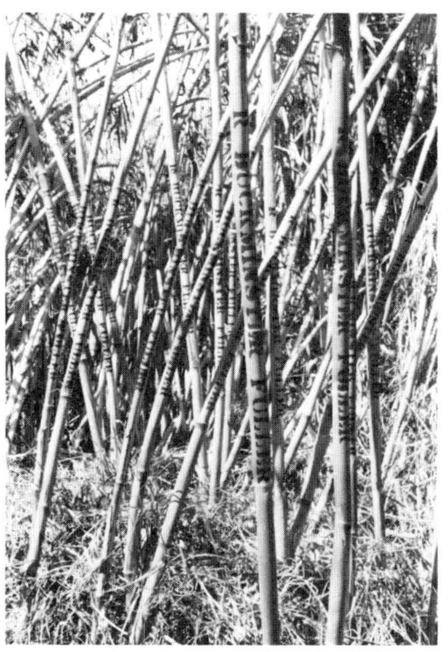

Fuller Forest, 1970
bamboo grove, ink
site work, Palos
Verdes, California

His intelligence was keen and explicit excitable but lazy. Again, perhaps, his idea or conviction of a life's finite circularity led to an innate lack of desire to close in conclusion his own visions. Therefore he lived a varied life—one rich in place and event. Yet one that paradoxically had the facts of a direction and the actuality of none. That the simultanity of these traits constantly existed in his life was not lost on Red Green. He seems to have resolved the dilemma by a belief that the circular linear wholeness of a life's continuum affected temporal event regardless. Perhaps in that sense he was a true embodiment of the democratic principle. This may be correct but still leaves a question posed—given his . . .

<hr>

[5]Jud Fine, *Ayers' Analog* text, 1974, as reproduced in *Jud Fine*, op. cit., 11. See also Madeleine Grynsztejn's entry on this work, p. 27.

[6]Cf. William D. Case, *Arts Magazine* (May, 1972): 72 ("engagingly direct"); Paul Stitelman, "Jud Fine," *Arts Magazine* (September, 1974): 40 ("cold and intellectual"); Lizzie Borden, "Cosmologies," *Artform* (August, 1972): 47 ("casual and off-handed"); Alan Moore, *Artforum* (April, 1975): 82–83 ("radically infracritical"); Peter Plagens, *Artforum* (November, 1973): 85–86 ("artiness on the cusp").

[7]For the source of this structure see Italo Calvino, *Mr. Palomar* (San Diego: Harcourt Brace Jovanovich, 1985), Index after page 126.

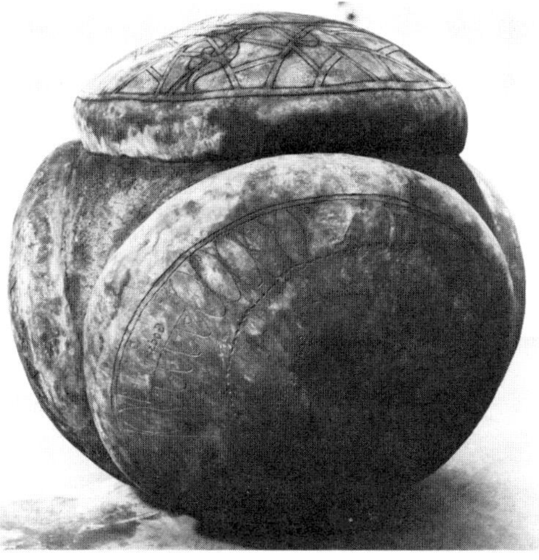

► *Neo,* 1987–88
cement, steel, wood,
bronze
54″ diameter
Courtesy the artist

►► *Annotation,*
1986–87
acrylic, charcoal, oil
pastel, pastel and ink
on canvas with
wood, oil stain, tar,
straw, string, steel,
stainless steel
9′9″ x 16′10″ x 12″
Courtesy the artist
and Ronald Feldman
Fine Arts,
New York City

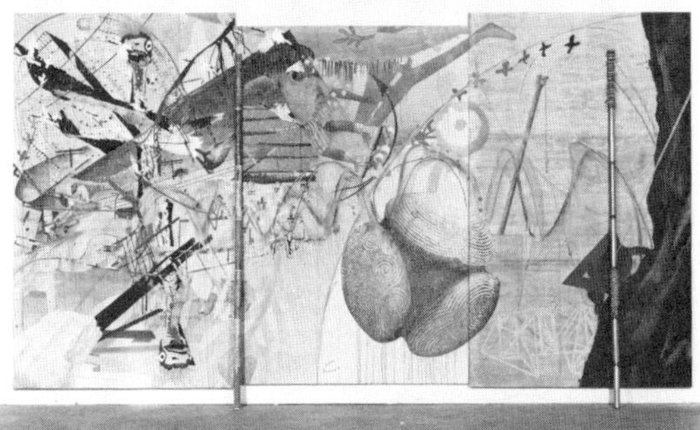

While Fine tells many tales in his visual work—from oceanic navigation systems, architectural history, and neolithic archeology to encounters with Buckminster Fuller, Ludwig Wittgenstein, and Claude Lévi-Strauss—none is formulated along the predictable lines of a story with a proper beginning, middle and end, a central subject, an identifiable narrative voice[8]

> *R/G as continuum: You see Red Green was his name—sometimes he would sign it R/G. Green is the male. Last name (surname) passed thru male. Slightly cold. Red, the female, came from his mother. Intellectually, red is slightly hot. A whole that is a functioning dualism of opposites (that is where opposition becomes a unity and in extension a producer). Red: A pullchain, a necklace of which the girl (Cheryl?) always wore. Rhythmic, pulsating, regularity—a regularity of blood. Heat. Green: Pungi stakes from an idea of a passive defensive aggression—idea of porcupine (a pungent pundit pedantically punctuating his pedestrian peculiarity—or, a sharp, biting and stimulating person of great learning narrow mindedly emphasized the trivial, piercing his ordinary, dull exclusive property). Bristling in antcipation as an entropy. Again: as an entropy. Cold.*

Instead, he treats his audience to a hybrid form where pictorial elements are interchangeable with words, where flow happens across a space (as in *Annotation*) as well as durationally through the act of reading. Instead of a clearly defined beginning, middle, end, with his layered matrix of images, we have an open-ended

---

[8]Many of Fine's concerns and inspirations, such as his reverence for Lévi-Strauss' *Tristes tropiques*, were recalled in discussions between the artist and this author over the past two years.

account that allows for a free-associational interpretation even as it remains fixed to a set of inspirational origins. It is as if Fine has found a way to mold the conventions of textual telling into the pliant formats associated with the nonsequential "reading" of visual representation.[9]

When fragments of a story are reordered according to other, non-temporal interests such as composition or color, as they are in a Fine pole, in an installation, painting or one of his book works, the telling of the story begins to shift towards a musical rather than a literary structure. Instead of a novel or a treatise, we might best regard a work like the cancelled *Math Text*, 1973, the graphic bulk text experiments (initiated in the mid-seventies) or *Annotation* as a score for a bold orchestration of words, numbers, and images from which we can elicit a variety of responses.

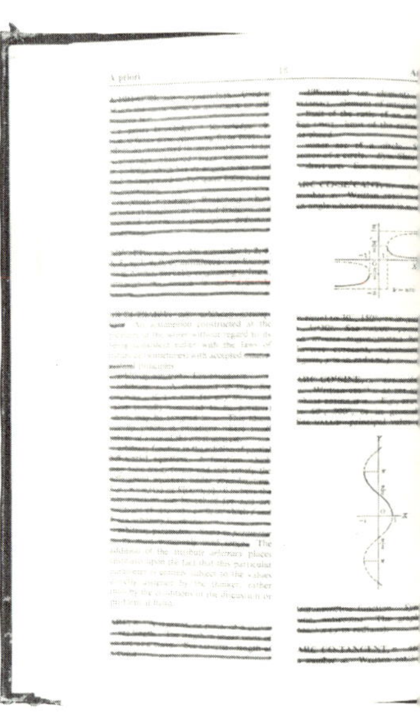

Red Green continuum: So who was the girl/woman? Her name tentatively reads as Verdican Rougette. Everybody called her "Verde" although she used to say "My American name is Cheryl." If this is true then, indeed, she signed all her graduate work "Cheryl Rougé." She was by her own statements part French and part Irish, but there was definitely a blood of the more southern climes in the mix to both explain the dark complexion and, more, the polar alternation of passive passion and violent, intense aggression. Bio: Appears as documented as a Phd. graduate student in Anthropology at Princeton in the early '70's. She, in a confluence of beauty and visionary competence, amasses a reputation as one of the potentially brightest in one of better Anthropology Departments in the country. She, as we have seen in previous discourse, decided to use herself as the objective of study for her anthropological leanings. Thus she became a subjective for her objective. An impossible role to pull, however, one not without interest in its attempt. As such she compiled a massive stack of writings, original and quoted, cited and dated sporadically and a series of obvious self-timer shot, poorly printed black and white 8x10's (with no accompanying negatives) of her committing various acts: planting corn in the asphalt, living in the caves of southern Crete and the now famous or infamous shots of her consuming the body of Red Green. This evidence arrived in a box with accompanning

---

[9] For more on narrative order see Nelson Goodman, "Twisted Tales; or Story, Study, and Symphony," *On Narrative*, 99–115.

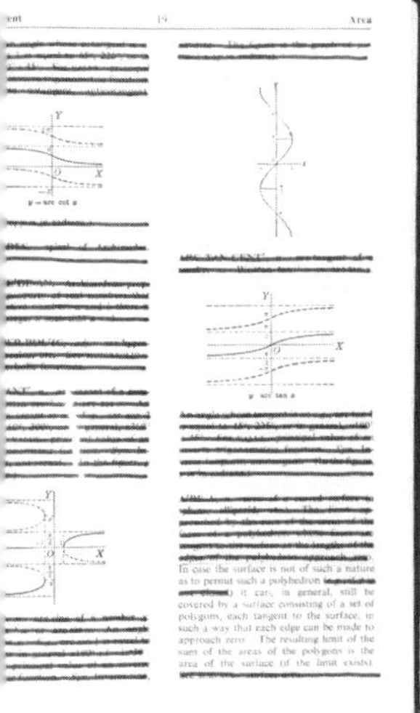

Math Text, 1973
clothbound book,
546 pages, magic
marker, pencil
9¼" x 6¼"
Courtesy the artist

The strong undercurrent of temporal concerns that is evoked by
many of Fine's images and the way he conveys them, parallel contemporary literary attitudes about the process of telling as well as
the readers' response:

> Reading is always this: there is a thing that is there, a thing
> made of writing, a solid, material object, which cannot be
> changed, and through this thing we measure ourselves
> against something else that is not present, something else
> that belongs to the immaterial, invisible world, because it can
> only be thought, imagined, or because it was once and is no
> longer, past, lost, unattainable . . . [10]

Fine's most masterful narration, and his most literary, while not
intended initially for public consumption, conflates his many
interests. Language, the difficulties of communication, the
exposure of the underlying assumptions in history, anthropology,
and biography and a kind of free-spirited, amusingly convoluted,
overworked plethora of information are all imbedded in the story
of Red Green. The semi-autobiographical character was con-
ceived in a notebook entry as a "Project called *Book*" with "real
words" which "would have as usual to do with everything and
nothing."[11]

His plans included a scheme to manipulate his "real words" freely,
misspellings and all, adding nuances and capabilities for language

---

[10] Italo Calvino, *If on a Winter's Night a Traveler*, 72.

[11] As published in *Jud Fine (Nothing New)* (Minneapolis: Dayton's Gallery 12, 1974).

to reveal and conceal, to expose reality and to create new realities.
He reminds himself:

> mix the language—punctuate—no punctuation—quotes—
> plagarize—original—leave out sources—make up sources—
> use dialect spellings—english spellings—misspellings—
> alternate spellings—announce all this and write it normal
> (always say red when you mean green)
>
> "Red is Green"
>
> An aside
>
> Color photograph of a red headed person (man) named
> green. "Red Green" "His name's 'Green' but we all called him
> 'Red.'"
>
> *Book*
>
> Fill in no particular order w/diagram fold/outs, drawings,
> original photographs, plagerized photographs, an occasional
> blank page, an occasional handwritten page![2]

What we have here, reminiscent of the kinds of physical process
lists created by Richard Serra in the sixties, is a plan for dissem-
bling the language and reconstituting it within a specific framework—the story of Red Green![3]

The contradictory complexity of Red Green—his name (neither
dumb nor smart), his character (both vague and well documented), his life (fictive with very real and even autobiographical
overtones), his discovery (historical record, perceptions of others,
literary sketch authored by visual artist), even his tense (a life
story of a dead man or a remaking of the author's own history)—is
a singular reflection of Fine's varied and infinite capacity to be
inclusive.

*(Realizing half way through his investigations that fascinat-
ing as it was, it would never hold as a doctoral desertation, he
concurrently and with little interest produced what has
become a standard of late century anthropological investigat-
ing form, a work on and entitled "The conditions pertaining
to . . . and consequence of . . . Mexican/Irish marriages:
1925–1955". It was this work that gained him the reputation
that resulted in his Phd. and his current position as the Chair
of Anthropological Strategies at Cornell Univ.) Mean while,
unrecognized academically* The R/G Continuum *became a
cult classic, movie rights pending. Verdican Rougette Aka*

---

[12]Jud Fine, artist's notebook journal entries dated from adjacent pages to October 1974.

[13]For the Serra list: "To Roll, To Crease, To Fold, To Stone, To Bend . . . ," See Gregoire Muller, *The New Avant-garde* (New York: Praeger Publishers, 1972), 94.

Like all his sculpture, paintings and drawings, Fine's story of "Rojo 'Red' Green" is part speculation and part documentation. To treat its subject matter more explicitly than its method is to misunderstand the intent of Fine's art and more importantly its effects. He defies focusing, singularity, and homogeneity for an aesthetic that compiles information *ad infinitum*. As such it is the perfect foil for the zen serenity of a minimalist aesthetic, as his work is engaged with the kind of sensory overload so typical of our information-driven society. Any painter who can compose a skateboarder, petroglyphs, a mountain climber, an ostrich, wave symbols, a neolithic stone, and "galloping gertie" (the famous self-destructive suspension bridge) onto a single canvas wants to effect, through the sheer volume of his voices and images. Fine's myriad voices are, after all, his most consistent characteristic; it is each individual work that stands before us on its own merits, each piece which arouses our curiosity and *not* the comparative connection to other examples.

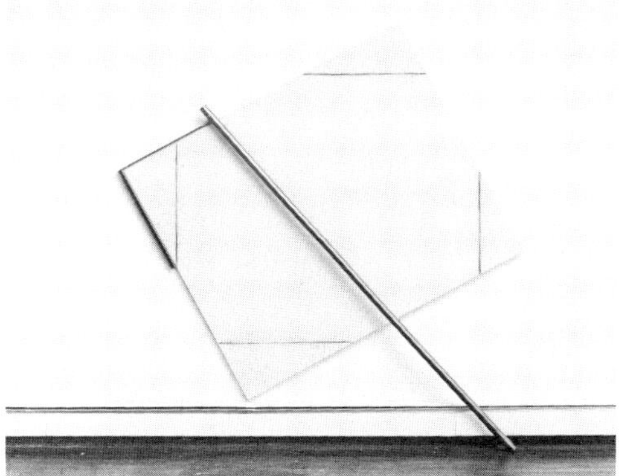

Living History,
1985
powdered pigment,
canvas, steel, wood
8' x 7'9" x 9"
Courtesy the artist

The question of Authorship. For instance who is writing this?

*Poe and Barth (***The Narrative of Arthur Gordon Pymn** *and* **Giles Goat Boy***) examples of an escaped identification as a responsibility. The idea of an entity that is strong enough or sets up a context in such a way so that it transcends (escapes identification with) its author. Have Jud Fine (the artist in Amsterdam) appear as himself. If I make the works that Jud Fine made in 1973, I remake my own history. A great lie—the consummate error is one done consciously that has consequence. If it can have consequence (that is external (to itself) effect (***Quantum Mechanics** *argument that all does (have effect) by definition—chance then being the foundation upon which pattern is built (deduced).....If it can have consequence (------"------), with full knowledge of its error, its lie, then consequence is one of content exposing its context—a label for which phenomenon might be "Living History" in which past/ present are seen as a synonymous simultaneity.*

Like all his art, from the early process pieces through the poles and structural works to his more recent hybrid mediums of painting and sculpture, Fine's primary interest, as that of any storyteller, is to set up a dialogue, to posit a set of assumptions that are carried through to some conclusion.

Idea of a staccato listing of events, narrations, descriptions, projections whose only literary trait is that they pull the reader along—meaning is a growing appreciation/comprehension of the situation which is not perceived as a linear structured narration whose author is always present, but as a non-structured, non-conclusive, circular addition—an attack as repetitive revelation of multi- (hence non-) authored information. This compilation of information attempts to locate its space in that area that is the initial time in research (focusing). At this point authorship is only defined by the focus—in that a glance contains the private property act of authorship—all else exists only as potential idea.

It is at this moment that the future author and the reader are in the same position—performing the same function.

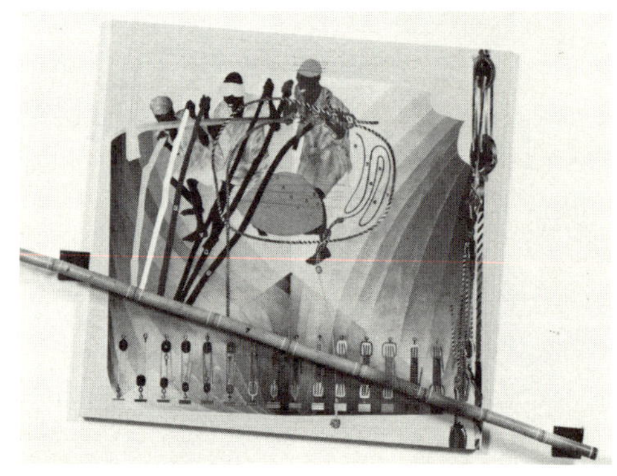

Co-Incident Weight,
1984
canvas, acrylic,
pencil, bamboo
5′10″ x 9′10″ x 6½″
Private Collection

It is then up to his audiences to draw inferences, conclusions, and respond accordingly. His work precipitates rather than resolves.

Like the primitive objects they may suggest to many of his viewers, Fine's sculptural objects are created more for participants and celebrants than for art audiences, viewers, curators, and collectors. Both his generic "primitive" sources and his intentional aestheticized objects are more like instruments of a ritual existence, some social interaction, to which a suitable response might be a grimace, a dance, a scream of fright, or a smile of delight. They engage despite rather than because of their obfuscation![14]

Idea of a surrogate from the fiberglass/steel bamboo—a maintenance of identity in spite of the presence of a stand-in that obviously is not synonymous with its referent. Red Green is not a stand-in for the author. Rather the author attempts to abdicate authorship in a similar fashion, by setting up a collaboration of form that defines a single identity that overlays and includes a replacement of material. (In the case of bamboo a linguistic/perceptive act in which the word "bamboo" defines both the form and the material. The word defines the form to such degree that the material can be altered and the definition still maintains. Again a simplistic case of a definition in which form overrides matter. In the latter instance the build-up of

---

[14]On the difficulties of making parallels between "primitive" and contemporary art, see Arthur Danto, " 'Primitivism' in 20th Century Art," *The State of the Art* (New York: Prentice Hall Press, 1987), 23–27.

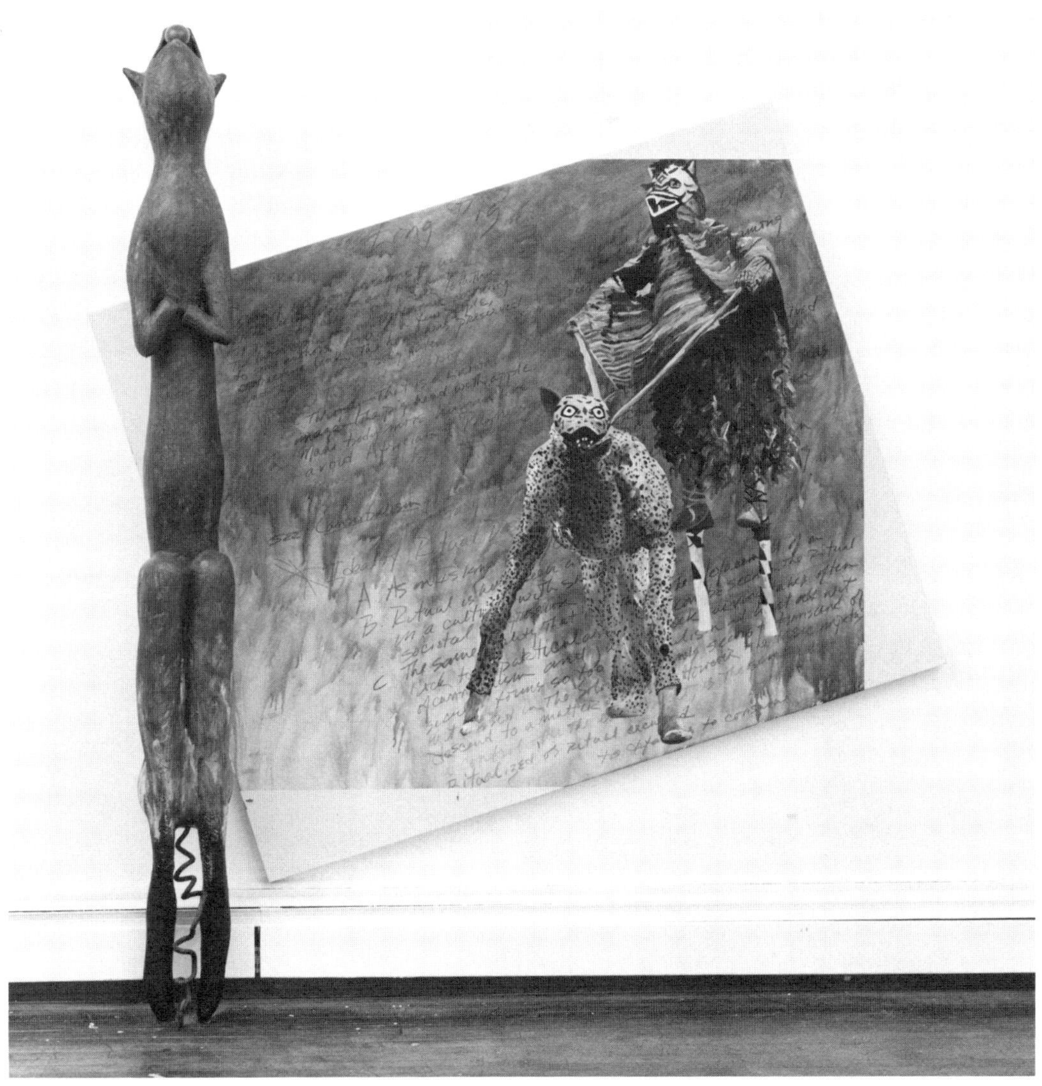

relational information maintains its uniqueness in the face of a confusion of (and thus the demise of the singularity of) authorship).

In the end Fine's most unique contribution is his direct and unwavering faith in the universality of his story and the power of his confirmed viewers to accomplish this essential collaboration. This is made literal and specific at the conclusion of the Red Green text as his narrator admits:

> Believe it or not—he believed in the essential integrity of the audience that this audience was potentially all inclusive race/breed/economic status, etc. and that its conception/formation participation was equal (on par with) to the author's.

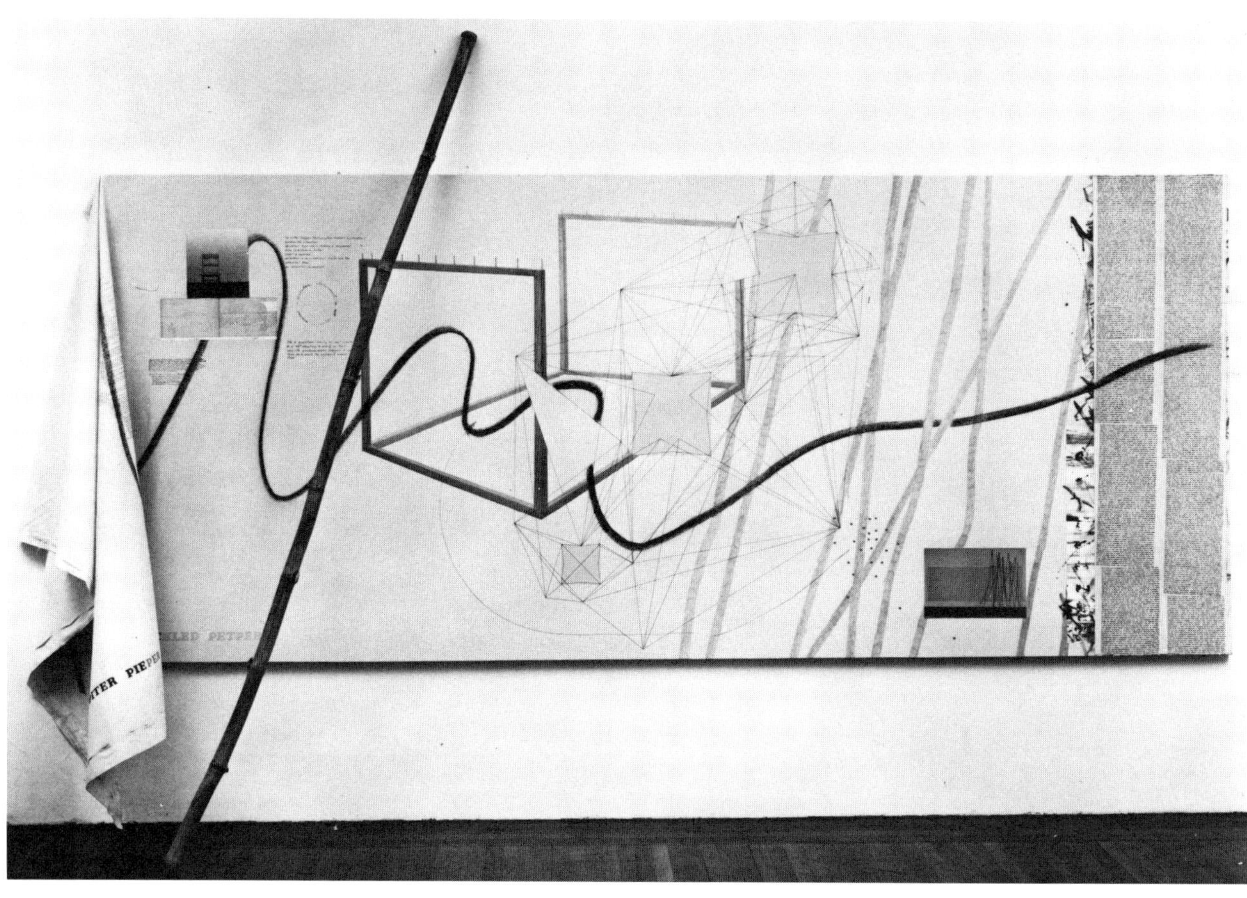

"__________," 1974, acrylic, ink, graphite, type, photograph, grommets, charcoal and collage on canvas, bamboo; canvas 5′ x 16′ on
a 5′ x 13′ frame; bamboo pole 9′6″ x 2″ diameter, Collection Yale University Art Gallery, Purchased with the Aid of Funds from the National
Endowment for the Arts and the Susan Morse Hilles Matching Fund

Commentaries:
Madeleine Grynsztejn

Jud Fine's first work on canvas, "____," is a summary of the images, issues, and directions indicated to him by his own art. Images derived from the artist's first exhibition, reproductions of Ayers Rock, photographs of obscure scientific experiments, and cryptic linguistic riddles reflect some of the privately held crosscurrents of the artist's personality and artistic influences. Fine also foregrounds the medium he employs and its conventions; thus, he uses all the attributes of a title without naming the work, while the raw canvas which is the ground for, but generally not the subject of, picture making plays an elegant sculptural role against the solid line of the leaning bamboo pole. Further, Fine takes as his starting point the quintessential "gestural" stroke, a sinuous charcoal line spanning the entire canvas, even as its refined, self-conscious elegance questions the very logic of "expression" which sees every mark as an index of the artist's interior state.

The line indifferently crosses over the canvas' right section where illegible typescript pages overlying expressive passages of color conflate the visual and the literal. From here the stroke weaves through the frozen penciled shadows of bamboo poles whose bodily counterparts are recorded in a photograph below, as they once leaned against "____." This effort to incorporate the perceptual and cognitive origins of an image, to record and present the process by which it was made, lies at the core of Fine's work, and finds its origins in early process art. In fact, within the drapery of excess canvas hanging from the work's left side is a bibliography which assiduously details this object's own sources (ranging from Marcel Duchamp to Joseph Kosuth). Linguistic proposition and physical fact thus appear within a single work which then acts as a kind of blueprint for itself; but Fine deliberately frustrates our full knowledge of this piece by making its primary sources of information physically inaccessible, since the "hidden meaning" of the work lies within the folds of an art object that cannot be unravelled.

Fine's work of the early seventies is informed by Minimalism and its later manifestations in process art. Thus *An Analogy* uses Minimalism's serial deployment of multiple and primary units. Insofar as these units reveal the method of their making they are process works, activated by the artist's manipulation of the material, and then constantly re-activated by the viewer who reconstructs the process involved in making the piece. *An Analogy* also exhibits the same uncompromising physicality, truth to material, and architectonic clarity that one finds in sculptures by post-Minimalist artists such as Richard Serra. Fine, however, completely departs from Minimalist tenets by using bamboo as a primary three-dimensional element—a simple and reduced form that nevertheless is inherently random, exhibiting the unique and unstable geometry of natural phenomena. Additionally, bamboo is loaded with strong and multivalent cultural references, and therefore necessarily involves the memories, associations, and behaviors of the viewer.

The poles in *An Analogy* recall ritualistic fetish objects, ceremonial South Sea artifacts, primitive weaponry, and elegantly crafted art totems. Anthropomorphic in their verticality, they also beg to be handled as one would a human artifact. This temptation to touch is encouraged by the casual, seemingly random arrangement of the individual poles: in fact, the notion of exhibition or display is underscored by the rack which mimics a commercial fishing pole display rack one would see in a sporting goods store. And to compound the commercial and arbitrary quality of presentation, the artist has attached to each pole a label resembling a price tag that bears the pole's individual title.

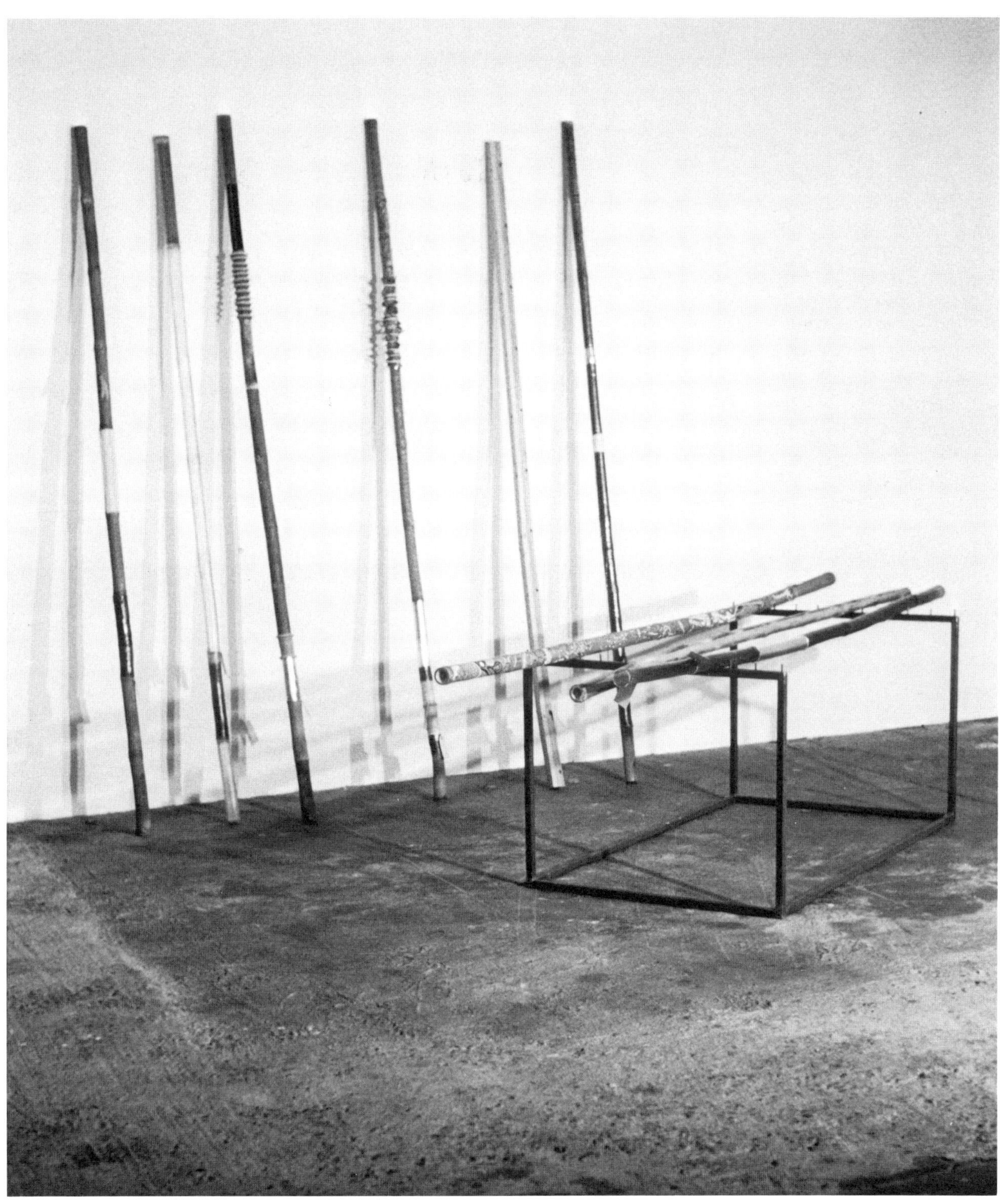

An Analogy, 1973, bamboo, steel, fiberglass, wood, mixed media, poles 9′6″ each, rack 36″ x 36″ x 60″, Collection The Art Institute of Chicago, 20th Century Purchase Fund

Annotation is Fine's most ambitious and complex work to date, a piece of epic scale and form. In the midst of an optical cross fire several of the composition's ordering devices are deduced and just as quickly reincorporated into the piece. While Fine uses the triptych structure, invested as it is with powerful art historical, even religious, connotations, he inverts its traditional form where the outer panels constitute the shorter portions of the piece. Not only does the middle panel "sink," but the poles leaning against the work disrupt and deny the canvas' tripartite division. These panels are optically joined by Fine's calculated gestural stroke (lifted from his own work, "__________"), which pulses across the composition's painstaking drawing and tight geometry. The overriding ordering device, however, is almost impossible to decipher: Fine uses the "golden rectangle" as his organizational tool, that system of bisections which in the High Renaissance determined the canvas size of "ideal" paintings. The lines of the golden rectangle are here extended to form the arc deflecting the skateboarder's advance as well as the sharp line dividing the ostrich from its reflection.

Within the network of these formal coordinates images float, fall and fly, products of Fine's environment, his culture, his voracious reading, his vicariousness, his media saturation. The artist's flight of fancy has as its subject, gravity: whether it is the falling weight of a Scottish neolithic rock or the painterly drips accentuating a downward direction. Intrinsic to gravity, space, too, is emphasized, conquered by bridge spans, navigated by an ancient Egyptian boat, or flown through by Japanese cranes. Indeed, various kinds of illusionistic spaces are exhibited simultaneously: the orthogonal grid of classical perspective; the indeterminate depth of geometric abstraction; the continuum of atmospheric landscape. At the work's upper left, aerial views of a bedouin community house overlie plans of Woodhenge; both resemble, indeed they are, fossils of a kind. As our eye moves across the work, the painterly, lush forms at left transform into the geometric, analytical drawing style at right: from what one observes in reality we move to the way one conceives of reality.

Fine involves the viewer in a creative, exploratory process as s(he) is required to walk, look, anticipate, and remember while the work continually changes and unfolds with every step. The dramatic, active movement generated within and outside this large visual field is a metaphor for human advancement and progression. By participating in the work, by confronting one's perceptions and exploring the paths revealed by *Annotation* the viewer discovers the complexity and meaning of the work, and ultimately shares in the excitement the artist himself derives from it.

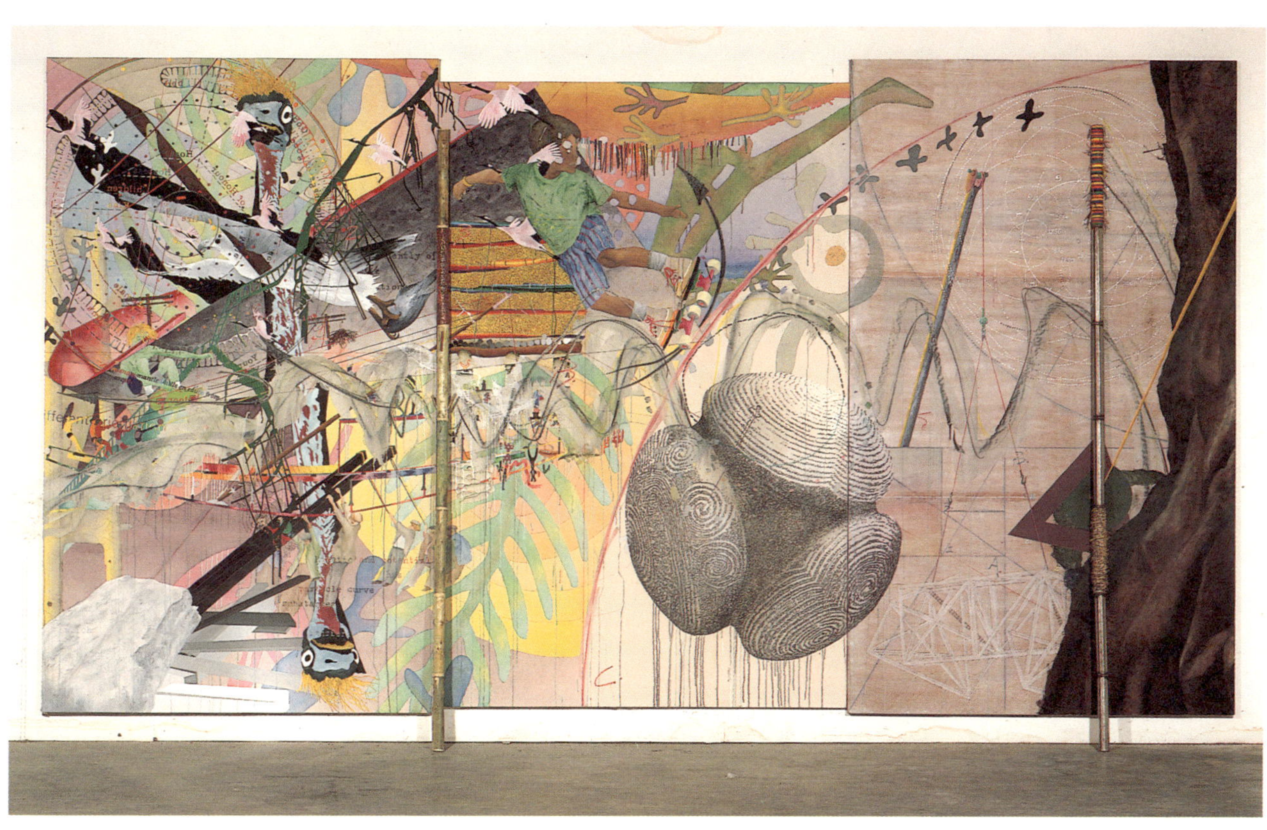

Annotation, 1986–87, acrylic, charcoal, oil pastel, pastel and ink on canvas with wood, oil stain, tar, straw, string, steel, stainless steel
9′9″ x 16′10″ x 12″, Courtesy the artist and Ronald Feldman Fine Arts, New York City

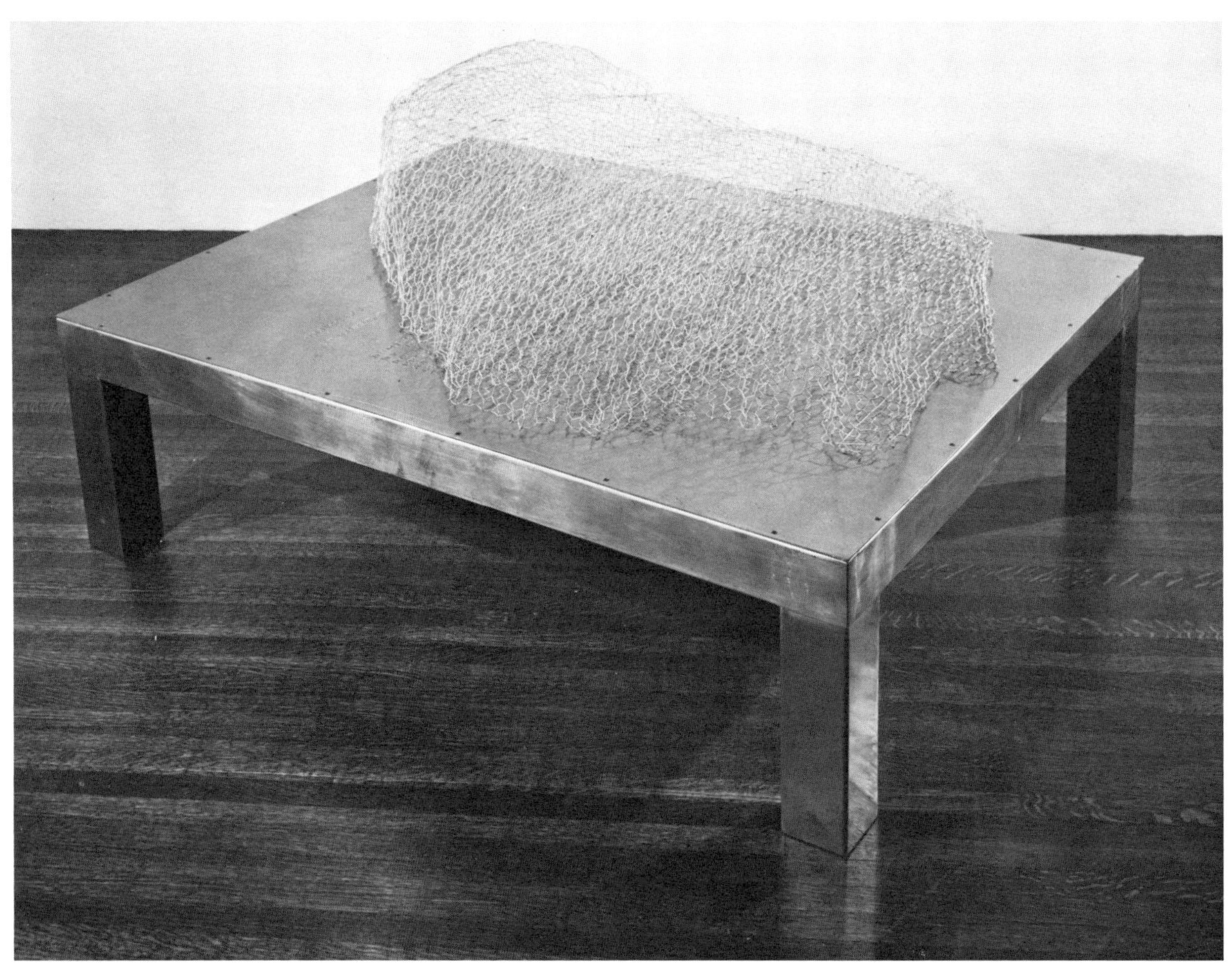

Ayers' Analog, 1974, steel, chicken wire, acid etched steel 36″ x 60″ x 48″, Collection Power Institute of Fine Arts, University of Sydney, Sydney, Australia

*A*yers' *Analog* operates as Jud Fine's model for the construction of meaning in sculpture. The object demonstrates the physical intersection of two different categories of information intrinsically related to the concept, "sculpture": the three-dimensional object, and its context. The primary source of this work, both visually and conceptually, is Ayers Rock, a dome-shaped monolith located in the western desert of southern Australia. As re-conceived by the Pitjandjara aborigines for whom this location is sacred, Ayers Rock is the source of their origin and their continued existence. Their collective beliefs explain the topography of Ayers Rock as being that of their totemic ancestors, transformed since the creation of the world into the rock's natural features. Thus the large boulders at Ayers Rock were once Pitjandjara women sitting in their camps, and the green lichen and black water stains are the transformed body decorations of old Liru men.

Fine's piece compounds this human propensity for naming and encoding the world around us by recomposing Ayers Rock as an abstract three-dimensional map, while adding his own conceptual strata. Between the quasi-Minimalist base recalling Australia's flat backlands and the chicken wire form whose amorphous edges describe Ayers Rock's continuous erosion, Fine inserts a text elucidating his own relationship to this site:

> **Ayers Rock as analogy is an occasion. The worth of the event is in its imaginative potential, since its logic is always false. It is therefore, in form, a possible triptych. Two physical elements and a connection. Two paradoxical conclusions and a physical fact. Two duration oppositions and a tension resolution.**
>
> **Corollary. How to preserve the steel against abuse from the wire, or converse how to preserve the object from abuse by the base, or inclusive how to preserve the fact against abuse from cultural evolution or exclusive how to preserve the present?**

While the viewer reads this acid-etched text through the chicken wire, the ghost-like replica of Ayers Rock is essentially annulled and replaced by the reader's private image of Ayers Rock, for one cannot see the sculpture and read the text simultaneously. For all the references to Ayers Rock, the landscape itself is strangely absent from the piece; instead, Fine creates for the viewer the experience of Ayers Rock literally read through the human subject, who has invested it with meaning. Like Robert Smithson's Nonsites, this work documents not only a place, but also the artist's involvement with the site, whether actual or imagined. As with the Nonsites, *Ayers' Analog* is nature reduced and abstracted to a dialogue between the site and its reconfiguration as sculpture.

His materials are rope, twine, nails, latex, resin, urine, wax, tar. . . . From
them he makes compact objects, formally intelligent in their tension
between a natural physicality and an elegant artificiality. Since 1981, the bamboo
pole which is Fine's leit-motif has been standardized to a height of 8 feet 9 inches.
Despite, or because of, his self-imposed, restricted grammar, Fine's *Watt/Analogy*
series has become ever more subtle and various with time, as these very param-
eters give rise to their own limitless variations.

Whether in their natural state or in their replication in copper, steel or fiberglass,
Fine's poles yield easily to the imprint of the action applied to them. Onto these
structures composed of natural divisions measuring between 12 and 18 inches,
Fine incises, paints, punctures, layers, nails, binds, and gilds in an obsessive,
laborious, almost ritualistic process. The materials are bound and confined,
rather than gestural; yet Fine's intuitive stresses, accents, and modulations serve
as vehicles for an intense and intimate experience.

The *Watt/Analogy* series is always presented very simply, weighted and canti-
levered against the floor and the wall, without the benefit of the welding typical of
Modernist or Cubist-derived sculpture. The poles are held in place solely by their
earnest response to the forces of gravity, resulting in a natural, if precarious, equi-
librium. These poles exhibit not the illusion of balance, but *actual* balance: they
do not disguise their physical properties, their weight and material, the fact that
they lean. The grouping of individual pieces abandons the hierarchical composi-
tional schemes of conventional sculpture, opting instead for Minimalism's lucid
order of "one thing after another." The effect of this unitary, repetitive system is
one of unified and unbounded expansion.

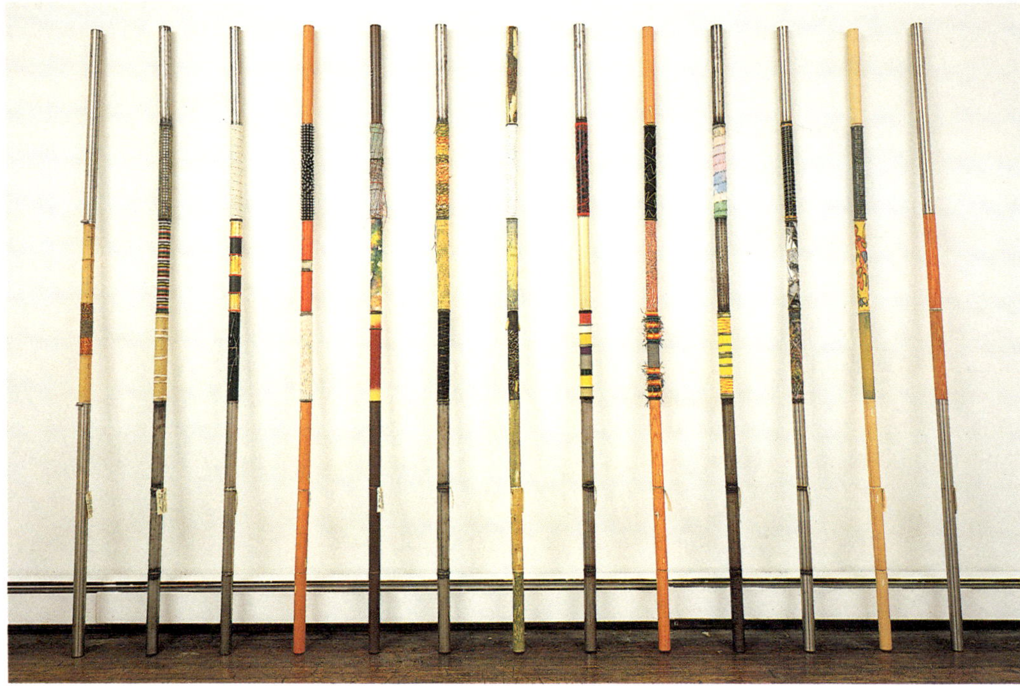

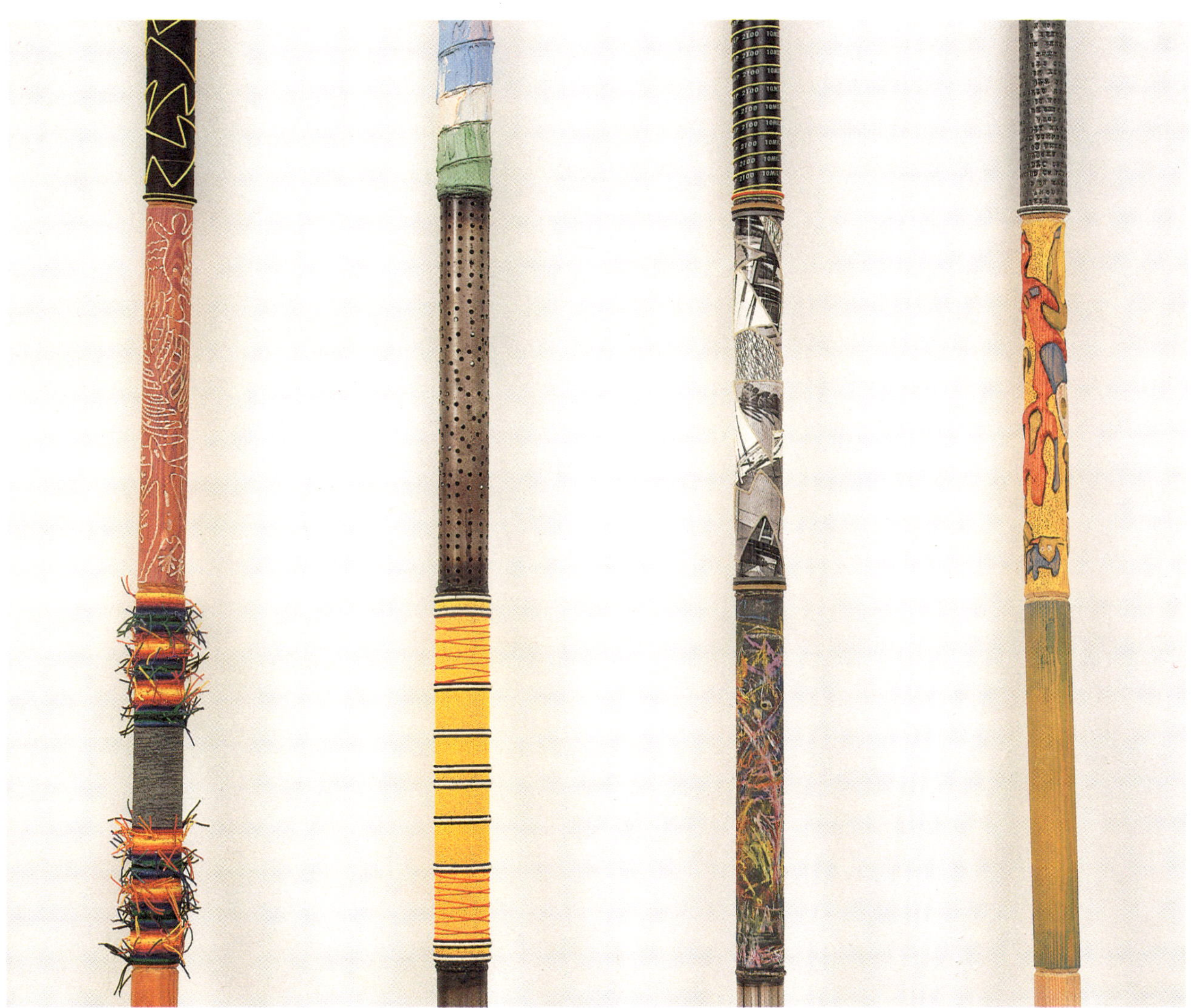

Poles from *Watt/Analogy* series, 1981–1987, mixed media on bamboo, steel, stainless steel, each pole 8'9" x 2" diameter, Courtesy Ronald Feldman Fine Arts, New York City

Exhibition Checklist

Height precedes width, width precedes depth

Corpuscle, 1971 (Rebuilt 1988)
chicken wire, string, bamboo
5'8" diameter x 14"
Courtesy the artist

Stut/Struss, 1972
chicken wire, rocks, string, bamboo
38" x 5'9" x 21"
Collection Los Angeles County
Museum of Art, Contemporary Art
Council, New Talent and Purchase
Award

Watt's Final Decision, 1972
bamboo, rubber latex, gold leaf,
fiberglass
poles 11'4" x 2" diameter
Collection the Museum of Contemporary Art, Los Angeles:
Gift of Alan Shayne

An Analogy, 1973*
bamboo, steel, fiberglass, wood,
mixed media
poles 9'6" each, rack 36" x 36" x 60"
Collection The Art Institute of
Chicago, 20th Century
Purchase Fund

Clear, 1973
ink, pencil, paper
60" x 9"
Courtesy Ronald Feldman Fine Arts,
New York City

Helix, 1973*
bamboo, fiberglass, rock
8'9" x 24" x 12"
Courtesy the artist

Los Angeles 1970, 1973
ink, pencil, photograph, paper
18" x 26"
Collection Riko Mizuno

Math Text, 1973
clothbound book, 546 pages, magic
marker, pencil
9 1/4" x 6 1/4"
Courtesy the artist

Mix Meta (Simi) Phor, 1973
photo, ink, paper
48" x 12'
Courtesy Ronald Feldman Fine Arts,
New York City

Primo Terce, 1973
fiberglass, photograph
photograph 18" x 18", poles 8'9" x 2"
diameter
Courtesy Ronald Feldman Fine Arts,
New York City

Yellow, 1973
fiberglass, wood, rock, bamboo,
enamel, gold leaf, steel, latex
pole 9' x 2" diameter, table form
32 1/2" x 32" x 44 3/4"
Collection Robert and Maryse Boxer,
London

"________," 1974*
acrylic, ink, graphite, type, photograph, grommets, charcoal and collage on canvas, bamboo,
canvas 5' x 16' on a 5' x 13' frame;
bamboo pole 9'6" x 2" diameter
Collection Yale University Art Gallery,
Purchased with the Aid of Funds from
the National Endowment for the Arts
and the Susan Morse Hilles Matching
Fund

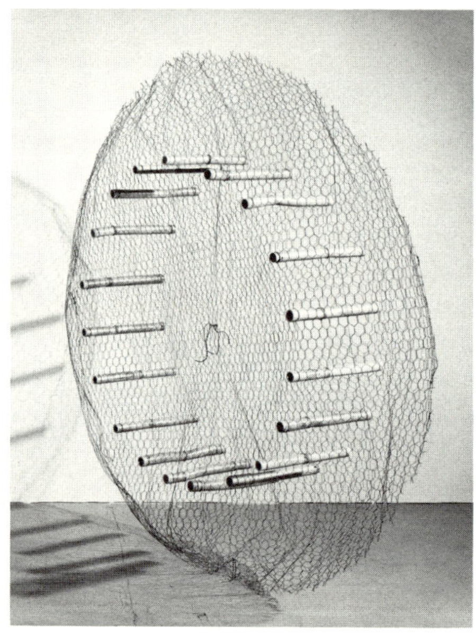

Corpuscle, 1971
(Rebuilt 1988)
chicken wire, string,
bamboo
5'8" diameter x 14"
Courtesy the artist

30

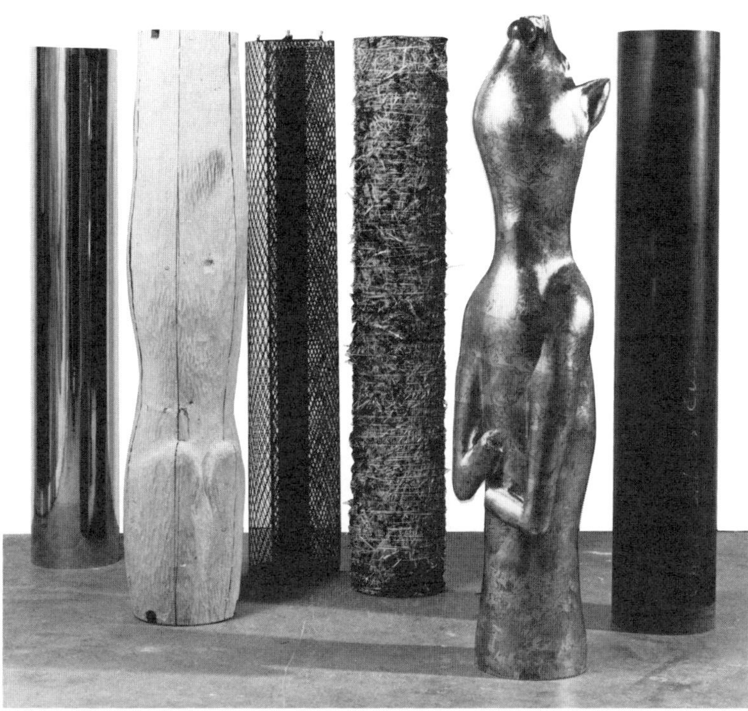

Dismembered (L.P.), 1987
tar, straw, string, steel,
nickel, hydra-cal, gold
leaf, wood 6 units each
5′10″ x 12″ diameter
Courtesy the artist and
Ronald Feldman Fine Arts,
New York City

Ayers' Analog, 1974 (Rebuilt 1988)
steel, chicken wire, acid etched steel
36″ x 60″ x 48″
Private Collection

Discourse, 1974 (edition of five)
saddle-stitched book, 8 pages
10 1/2″ x 7 1/2″
Self-published, courtesy the artist

Wak.x, 1974*
steel, plexiglass, copper, wax,
waxbean
60″ x 60″, pole 8′9″ x 2″ diameter
Collection the Museum of Contemporary Art, Chicago: Gift of the Century
America Corporation, Chicago, courtesy William J. Hokin

Confessions (detail), 1976
pencil, colored pencil, paper
each of 108 drawings 17 1/2″ x 23″ in 4
panels 2 - 60″ x 60″,
2 - 60″ x 20″
Collection Robert and Maryse Boxer,
London

Impology, 1977*
etched cadmium coated steel, string,
masking tape, wood
60″ x 60″
Collection the Museum of Contemporary Art, Chicago: Gift of William J.
Hokin

A Narrative Sculpture, 1978
steel, paper, ink, colored ink
48″ x 7″, pole 8′9″ x 2 1/2″ diameter
Collection Charles Hack

Error from Watt/Analogy, 1979
watercolor on canvas, string, marking
pen on fiberglass pole construction
8′8 3/4″ x 2 ″ diameter
Collection Margo H. Leavin

Bound from Watt/Analogy, 1980
mixed media on wood pole
8′9″ x 2″ diameter
Collection Sue and Steven Antebi

Try from Watt/Analogy, 1980*
mixed media on fiberglass pole
8′9″ x 2 ″ diameter
Collection Sue and Steven Antebi

Tertiary #1, 1981*
watercolor, pencil, paper
60″ x 40″, 60″ x 13′9″ in 4 panels
Collection The Capital Group, Inc.

Horizontal Pillar #8, 1982-88*
steel, wood, copper, stainless steel,
enamel
80′ x 9″ diameter
Courtesy the artist in conjunction
with Margo Leavin Gallery

Read, 1982*
chicken wire, etched stainless steel,
straw, acrylic, pencil, ink, canvas,
wire, string
60″ x 13′ x 8″
Courtesy the artist

Conjecture from Watt/Analogy, 1983*
mixed media on stainless steel pole
8′9″ x 2″ diameter
Collection Sue and Steven Antebi

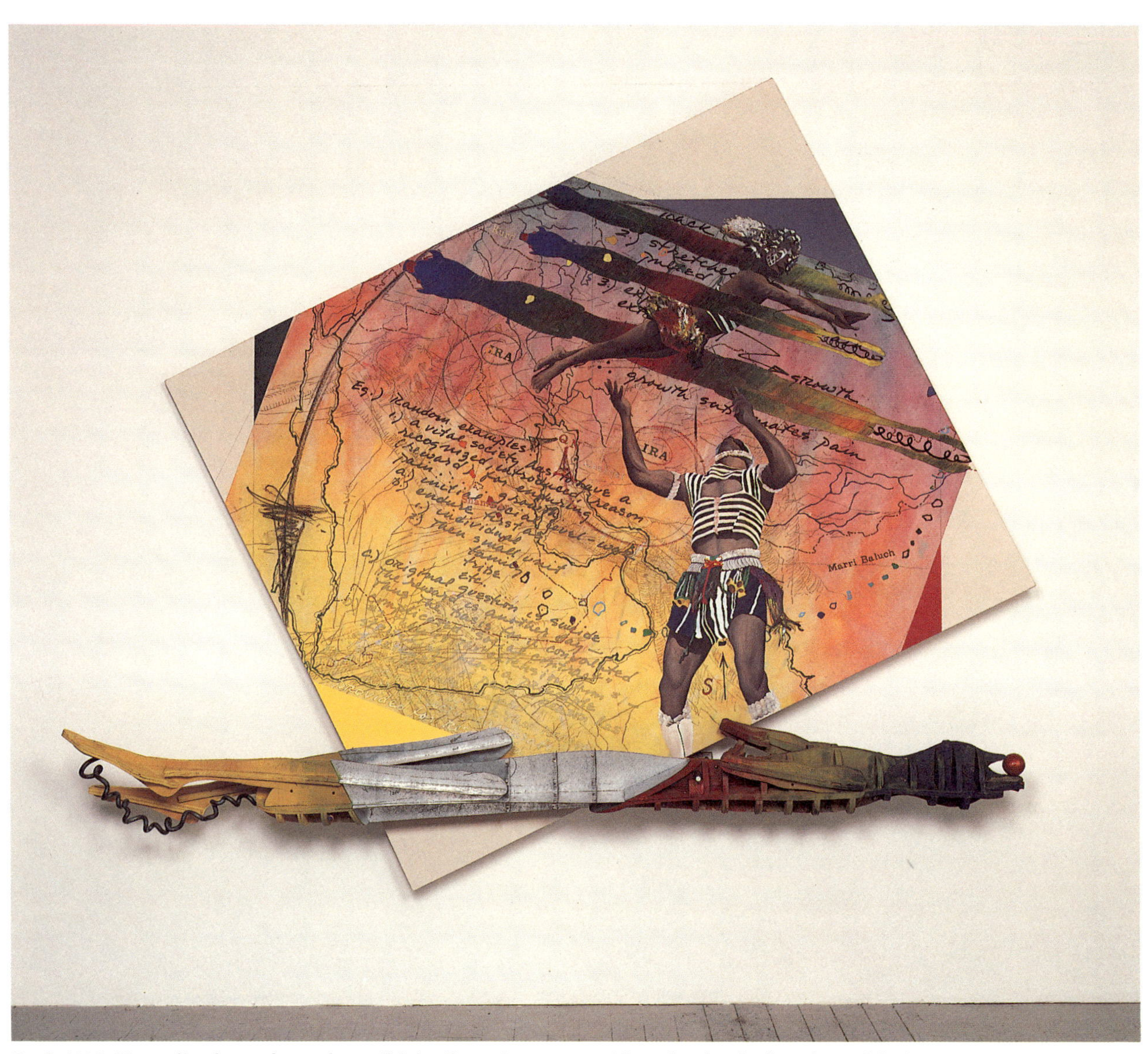

Rack, 1987–88, acrylic, charcoal, pastel, pencil, ink, oil pastel on canvas with steel, galvanized steel, wood, hydra-cal, encaustic, truss 8′ x 8′ x 14″, Courtesy the artist

Occupation from Watt/Analogy, 1983
mixed media on stainless steel pole
8′9″ x 2″ diameter
Collection Sue and Steven Antebi

Slice from Watt/Analogy, 1983*
mixed media on bamboo pole
8′9″ x 2″ diameter
Collection Sue and Steven Antebi

OR from Watt/Analogy, 1984
mixed media on bamboo
8′9″ x 2″ diameter
Collection Susan and Bill Ehrlich

Dbl. OR, 1985
oilstick, oil paint, acrylic, graphite, ink, colored ink, prisma stick, bamboo, chicken wire, steel, stainless steel, wood, canvas
6′10″ x 13′, column 8′ x 12″ diameter
Collection Santa Barbara Museum of Art: Gift of Barry and Gail Berkus

Living History, 1985*
powdered pigment, canvas, steel, wood
8′ x 7′9″ x 9″
Courtesy the artist

Annotation, 1986-87
acrylic, charcoal, oil pastel, pastel and ink on canvas with wood, oil stain, tar, straw, string, steel, stainless steel
9′9″ x 16′10″ x 12″
Courtesy the artist and Ronald Feldman Fine Arts, New York City

Precedent from Watt/Analogy, 1986
mixed media on steel pole
8′9″ x 2″ diameter
Collection Susan and Bill Ehrlich

Round, 1986
charcoal, canvas, wood, oil stain, steel, stainless and galvanized steel
8′ x 7′7″ x 5′10″
Courtesy the artist

Silenced from Watt/Analogy, 1986
string, ink, rubber, wood, acrylic on stainless steel pole
8′7½″ × 1⅞″
Collection Federal Reserve Bank of San Francisco, Los Angeles Branch

Stack from Watt/Analogy, 1986*
mixed media on bamboo pole
8′9″ x 2″ diameter
Collection Marshall and Patricia Geller

That's from Watt/Analogy, 1986*
mixed media on steel pole
8′9″ x 2″ diameter
Collection Marshall and Patricia Geller

Cut from Watt/Analogy, 1987
mixed media on bamboo, steel, stainless steel
8′9″ x 2″ diameter
Courtesy Ronald Feldman Fine Arts, New York City

Dismembered (L.P.), 1987
tar, straw, string, steel, nickel, hydra-cal, gold leaf, wood
4 units each 5′10″ x 12″ diameter
Courtesy the artist and Ronald Feldman Fine Arts, New York City

Long Pig, 1987*
pastel and acrylic on canvas, hydra-cal, steel, wood, encaustic
8′1″ x 7′4″ x 16″
Courtesy the artist and Ronald Feldman Fine Arts, New York City

Long Pig II, 1987
steel, wood, nickel-plate, hydra-cal, encaustic
23′4″ x 12″ diameter
Courtesy the artist and Ronald Feldman Fine Arts, New York City

Neo, 1987-88
cement, steel, wood, bronze
54″ diameter
Courtesy the artist

Never from Watt/Analogy, 1987
mixed media on steel pole
8′9″ x 2″ diameter
Collection Susan and Bill Ehrlich

Rack, 1987-88
acrylic, charcoal, pastel, pencil, ink, oil pastel on canvas with steel, galvanized steel, wood, hydra-cal, encaustic, truss
8′ x 8′ x 14″
Courtesy the artist

*Indicates work on view at La Jolla venue only

Chronology

November 20, 1944, born to June and Jack Fine in Los Angeles, California

1962
Graduates from Mira Costa High School, Manhattan Beach, California.

1962-64
Studies at El Camino College, Gardena, California; mathematics major, changes to history.

1964-67
Studies at the University of California, Santa Barbara, receiving a B.A. in American history. Continues graduate studies in American intellectual history. As assistant to Dr. Harold Kirker, researches historiography of recent American cultural history and early California artists. Assists in final drafts of book on Charles Bulfinch, Boston architect. Researches African oral tradition on English explorer Sir Samuel Baker from the viewpoint of the Bantu people of Lower Sudan, Africa. Takes courses in ceramics, painting, and sculpture.

1968-70
Studies at Cornell University, Ithaca, New York, in the graduate school's sculpture department, where he earns an M.F.A. Holds position as teaching assistant, running the fiberglass shop and teaching course in basic drawing for architects. Produces master's thesis exhibition of models and plans for proposed large-scale projects on remote bodies of water.

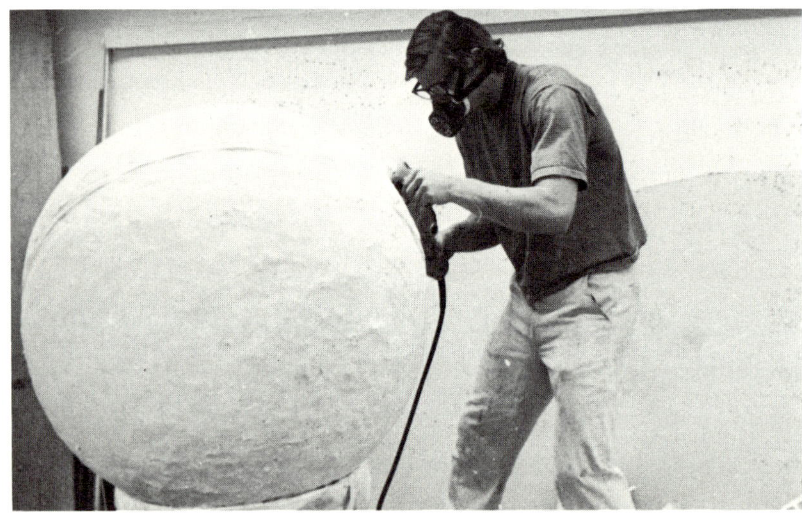

Working on *Zipper,*
1968

1970-71
Moves back to California. Instructor at Los Angeles Harbor College, teaches ceramics, perspective drawing, and lecture course on contemporary art.

In Venice studio, works on film scripts and begins independent anthropological studies/activities. Travels to Baja, Mexico; constructs earth works, explores issues of real time, the hand-made, and the site-specific. This work is later continued in the Santa Monica mountains.

1972

Inaugurates sculpture courses, design classes at Los Angeles Harbor College where he introduces video and 8 mm film as sculptural and three-dimensional design elements. Begins to make work in large adjacent swamp. Studio burns down; all tools are stolen; continues to use shell and begins first works using bamboo, rocks, chicken wire, and string. Early work, it is informed by Minimalist movement in the reduction of the object to its basic components (structure, surface, hooking device), while using natural elements antithetical to Minimalism.

First solo exhibition, Riko Mizuno Gallery, Los Angeles.

Solo exhibition, Ronald Feldman Fine Arts, New York City (henceforth, exhibits at Feldman almost annually); shows rock and string wall works, latex and bamboo pieces, poles, and works using string, bamboo, chicken wire, and rock.

Exhibits three works at Documenta 5, Kassel, West Germany, including first vertical bamboo pole series. Travels to Germany and Italy. Participates in "Looking West," ACA Gallery, New York; "Sculptors' Drawings," Margo Leavin Gallery, Los Angeles; "5 L.A. Artists," San Francisco Art Institute; "Attitudes '72," Pasadena Museum of Art, California.

Receives Los Angeles County Museum of Art New Talent Award.

1973

Constructs large studio in Santa Monica.

For solo exhibition at Brand Art Center, Glendale, California, makes ten works using rocks, chicken wire, string, and bamboo as basic structural elements. Participates in "The Wall Object," La Jolla Museum of Contemporary Art; "8th Biennale de Paris," Musée d'Art Moderne de la Ville de Paris.

Writes *OR: An Introduction* in which he defines a language that is both visual and verbal.

1974

Travels to Europe for six months. Visits Milan, Munich, works one month in Amsterdam, spends two months in southern Crete. Executes large work in Pescara, Italy, at Lucrezia de Domizio gallery. At Edinburgh Summer Art Festival, Scotland, exhibits an installation and *Decision*, a written work.

Begins collaboration with Ian Hamilton Finlay. Produces about forty drawings, two concrete "tot walls" in northern Scotland, a number of granite works, and embroideries. These works exhibited in London and Australia.

Solo exhibition, Dayton's Gallery 12, Minneapolis, Minnesota. Constructs a vertical, large-scale outdoor pole, *Whitney Prop*, exhibited against the back wall of the Whitney Museum of American Art, New York. Makes *Ayers' Analog*, first work to incorporate literary narrative and criticism.

Included in "Seven Sculptors' New Involvement with Materials," Institute of Contemporary Art, Boston; "71st American Exhibition," The Art Institute of Chicago. Visiting lecturer at The Art Institute of Chicago where he receives the Laura Slobe Memorial Award.

Publishes *OR: An Introduction*.

1975

June—arrives in Comptche, California. Builds house on twenty-six acres in Mendocino County. Six months' suspension of artistic activities. Spends two months in Mexico.

Solo exhibit at Galerie Alexandra Monett, Brussels, Belgium. Participates in "Primitive Presence in the '70s," Vassar College Art Gallery, Poughkeepsie, New York; "Word/Number Image," Sarah Lawrence College, Bronxville, New York; "Drawings—U.S.A.," Stadtisches Museum, Leverkusen, West Germany.

1976

Sculptor in Residence, The Art Institute of Chicago.

Moves to Carpinteria, California.

Makes *Confessions*, 108 drawings, each containing written text and images positing art in the future as a secular religion.

Participates in "Drawing/Disegno," Cannaviello Studio d'Arte, Rome. "Painting and Sculpture Today '76," Indianapolis Museum of Art, Indiana.

Publishes *Walk*, based on concepts developed in Europe and executed in Lancaster, California.

1977

Lecturer, University of California, Santa Barbara. Begins teaching at the University of Southern California, Los Angeles.

Solo exhibition at Margo Leavin Gallery, Los Angeles (subsequent exhibitions in 1979, 1981, 1982, 1984). Shows first *Boxstorms*, works that extend concepts of analogy to include primary as well as secondary information, and the possibility of misinformation.

Executes first watercolors for exhibition, "Watercolors and Related Media by Contemporary Californians," at Baxter Art Gallery, California Institute of Technology, Pasadena.

Exhibits at Marianne Deson Gallery, Chicago; Art Gallery, California State University, Fullerton (includes a retrospective survey catalogue of work from 1970 to 1976).

Participates in "Words at Liberty," Museum of Contemporary Art, Chicago; "View of a Decade," Museum of Contemporary Art, Chicago.

1978

Builds studio in Carpinteria, California, for which he designs a truss system for ceiling rafters. This subsequently influences large-scale works (*Tripoli*, 1979, *Split*, 1979, *Relay*, 1980).

Lives in New York City for three months.

Solo exhibition at the Los Angeles Institute of Contemporary Art (LAICA) constitutes a survey of the works' structural development. Shows first single pole, *Dogshit to Diamonds*, and first standard-size pole, *Helix*. Large-scale works shown in "Three Sculptors," Santa Barbara Museum of Art, California.

Receives Art in Public Places Grant from the National Endowment for the Arts through the Santa Barbara Arts Forum to construct a permanent outdoor sculpture for the city of Santa Barbara.

1979

Travels to Hawaiian island of Kauai. Initiates investigations of Polynesian navigation.

Visiting artist, sculpture department, solo exhibition, College of Creative Studies, University of California, Santa Barbara.

Solo exhibition at Margo Leavin Gallery, Los Angeles; first navigation works contrast Polynesian navigation, a primary system, with celestial navigation, a secondary system, to generate tertiary thinking, a method for solving the dilemmas presented in both systems of navigation.

Relay shown at "10 Sculptors/15 Works: Outdoors," California State College, San Bernardino; subsequently permanently installed in Santa Barbara (1981).

Participates in "Aspects of Abstract: Recent West Coast Abstract Painting and Sculpture," Crocker Art Museum, Sacramento, California.

1980

Visiting associate professor, University of Southern California, Los Angeles.

Moves to downtown Los Angeles and begins renovation on 5,500 square-foot raw loft space.

Initiates investigation of archaic architectural archetypes, opposing the grass bundle of East Asia (*Shime*) to the stone circles of Northern Europe (*Stone*), resulting in *Horizontal Pillar #1*, a 160′ long horizontal cylinder constructed of straw, steel, and wire. Exhibited in "Architectural Sculpture: Projects," Baker Art Gallery, California Institute of Technology, Pasadena.

Exhibits at the Los Angeles Institute of Contemporary Art (LAICA); participates in "Sculpture in California, 1975-1980," San Diego Museum of Art, California.

1981

Ronald Feldman Gallery's new 6,000 square-foot gallery space allows for first exhibition of Fine's large-scale work in New York City. Exhibits *Shime/Stone*, continuing opposition of archaic Eastern and Western architecture; *Navigation*, exploring primary, secondary, and tertiary systems of navigational information.

Participates in "Messages, Words and Images," Freedman Gallery, Albright College, Reading, Pennsylvania; "Polychrome," Hansen Fuller Goldeen Gallery, San Francisco; "Downtown Los Angeles," Madison Art Center, Madison, Wisconsin.

Records "Polynesian/Polyhedron" at Green Street Recording Studios, New York City, for "Revolutions: the Art Record," a double 33 1/3 rpm album.

1982

Assistant professor, University of Southern California, Los Angeles.

Purchases and renovates residence in Santa Monica; maintains studio downtown.

Solo exhibition at Anderson Gallery, Virginia Commonwealth University, Richmond; Dart Gallery, Chicago. Participates in "Security Pacific Collection," Los Angeles Municipal Art Gallery; "100 Years of California Sculpture," Oakland Museum of Art, California; "Exchange Between Artists, 1931-1982," Musee d'Art Moderne de la Ville de Paris, France.

Constructs *Horizontal Pillar #5*. Constructs second, permanent installation as part of exhibition, "Sculpture Sacramento," commissioned by the Sacramento Metropolitan Arts Commission for the city of Sacramento, California.

Receives National Endowment for the Arts Individual Artist Fellowship in sculpture.

1983

Associate professor, University of Southern California, Los Angeles.

Sells residence in Santa Monica. Leases and renovates 6,000 square-foot raw space in Venice, California.

Solo exhibition, Thomas Segal Gallery, Boston; Margo Leavin Gallery, Los Angeles; exhibits first paintings/drawings that attempt to isolate the image from its canvas ground by tilting the picture plane.

Participates in "Young Talent Awards: 1963-1983," Los Angeles County Museum of Art.

1984

Spends summer in New York City. Travels in the fall to the Yucatan, Mexico, and the Virgin Islands.

Participates in "Art of the States," Santa Barbara Museum of Art, California; "California Sculpture Show," Fisher Gallery, University of Southern California, Los Angeles (traveling exhibition); "Japanese-American Affinities," Los Angeles Municipal Art Gallery, Barnsdall Park, California.

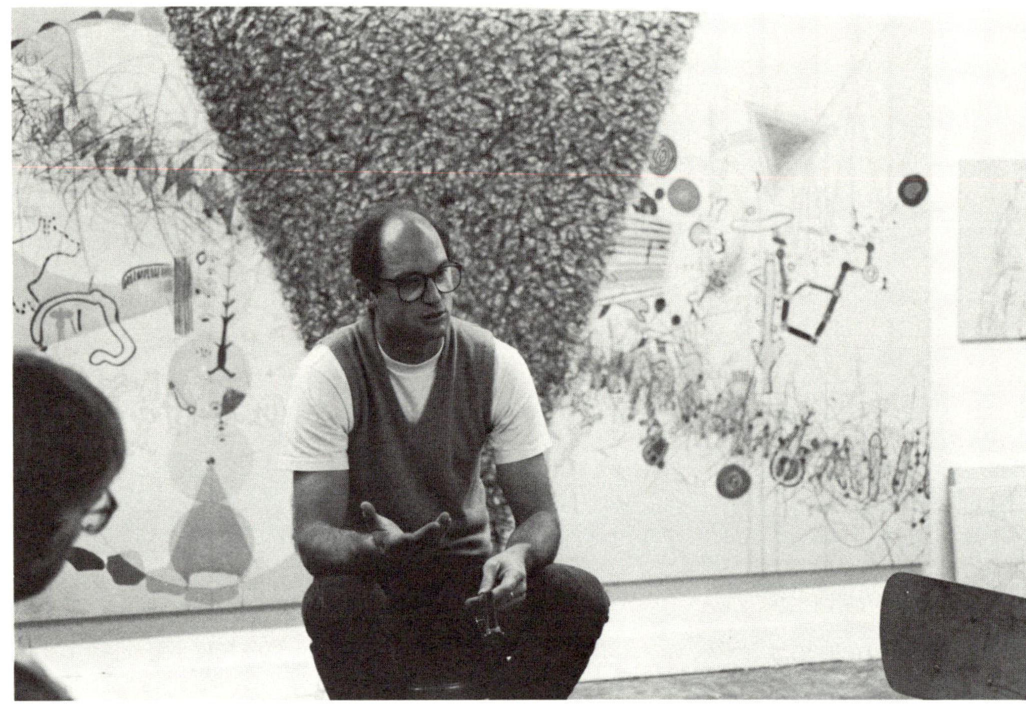

Jud Fine

1985

Travels to the Yucatan, Mexico.

Installs "A Physical Narration without Plot," Installation Gallery, San Diego, California.

Comprehensive solo exhibition, Los Angeles Municipal Art Gallery, Barnsdall Park, California, with accompanying catalogue, *Jud Fine: February 1985*. Participates in "Selections from the William J. Hokin Collection," Museum of Contemporary Art, Chicago; "Out of the Ooo Cloud: Artists Salute the Return of Halley's Comet," Edith C. Blum Art Institute, Bard College and Light Gallery, Annandale-on-Hudson, New York.

1986

Visiting professor, San Diego State University, San Diego, California.

Completes separate studio/living space in Carpinteria, California.

Participates in "1976-1986: Ten Years of Collecting Contemporary American Art," Wellesley College Museum, Wellesley, Massachusetts; "A Southern California Collection," Cirrus Gallery, Los Angeles; "Drawing for Sculpture," Thomas Segal Gallery, Boston; "Representational Images in Contemporary Art," Carpenter/Hochman Gallery, Dallas, Texas; Thomas Babeor Gallery, La Jolla, California.

1987

Purchases and begins renovation on studio building in downtown Los Angeles. Summer in Carpinteria studio.

Solo exhibition, Thomas Babeor Gallery, La Jolla, California; "Divine Hunger," Ronald Feldman Gallery, New York City, where he exhibits new work on sublimated mortuary cannibalism. Participates in "Models and Concepts of the Arena: Museum of Seasonal Change," Imperial Bank Building, San Diego, California; "The Capital Group: Selections from a Corporate Collection," Fine Art Gallery, University of California, Irvine, California.

Bibliography

1972

Attitudes '72. Exhibition catalogue. Pasadena, California: Pasadena Museum of Art.

Documenta 5. Exhibition catalogue. Kassel, West Germany: Museum Fridericianum.

Kurtz, Bruce. "Documenta 5: A Critical Preview." *Arts Magazine* (Summer): 32.

Tuchman, Maurice. *Art Council Acquisitions*. Exhibition catalogue. Los Angeles: Los Angeles County Museum of Art.

1973

8th Biennale de Paris. Exhibition catalogue. Paris, France: Musée D'Art Moderne de la Ville de Paris, Idea Books.

McCann, Cecile N. "Cross-Culture Vanguard Art." *Artweek*, October 6, 4.

Plagens, Peter. "Review: Los Angeles, Jud Fine, Riko Mizuno Gallery." *Artforum* (November): 85.

Stitelman, Paul. "New York Galleries." *Arts Magazine* (December): 60.

Tarshis, Jerome. "National Scene, L.A. Section." *Art News* (November): 107.

1974

Jud Fine (Nothing New). Minneapolis, Minnesota: Dayton's Gallery 12.

Fine, Jud. *OR: An Introduction*. New York: Ronald Feldman Fine Arts and Minneapolis, Minnesota: Dayton's Gallery 12.

Speyer, A. James. *71st American Exhibition*. Exhibition catalogue. Chicago: The Art Institute of Chicago.

Stitelman, Paul. "Jud Fine." *Arts Magazine* (September): 40-42.

1975

Print Collectors Newsletter (July-August).

Word/Number Image. Exhibition catalogue. Bronxville, New York: Sarah Lawrence College.

Barrio-Garay, Jose L. "Cronica de Nueva York." *Goya* (July/August): 39-44.

Frackman, Noel. "Arts Reviews." *Arts Magazine* (March): 6.

Kramer, Hilton. "Art: Seeing an Emotion's Shape." *New York Times*, January 11, 21.

Moore, Alan. "Arts Reviews." *Artforum* (April): 82.

Turnbull, Betty. *A Drawing Show*. Exhibition catalogue. Newport Beach, California: Newport Harbor Art Museum.

Wedewer, Rolf. *Drawings—U.S.A.* Exhibition catalogue. Leverkusen, West Germany: Stadtisches Museum.

1976

Cristin, Lilli. *Art U.S.A.: Southern California*. Exhibition catalogue. Fukuaka, Japan: American Center.

Fine, Jud. "Discourse." *Tracks: A Journal of Artists' Writing* (Spring).

__________. *Walk*. Chicago: Self-published.

Frackman, Noel. "Review." *Arts Magazine* (June): 19.

Greenleaf, Anne. *Painting and Sculpture Today '76*. Exhibition catalogue. Indianapolis, Indiana: Indianapolis Museum of Art.

Kramer, Hilton. "Art: Ammi Phillips' Children Steal a Show." *New York Times*, April 17, 16.

Wilson, William. "Muddied on Philosophy's Turf." *Los Angeles Times*, September 20, Part IV, 4.

1977

Watercolors and Related Media by Contemporary Californians. Exhibition catalogue. Pasadena, California: Baxter Art Gallery, California Institute of Technology.

Frankel, Dextra. *Jud Fine: Confessions and Related Works 1970–1976*. Exhibition catalogue. Fullerton, California: Art Gallery, California State University, Fullerton.

Friedman, Martin, Peter Gay and Robert Pincus-Witten. *View of a Decade*. Exhibition catalogue. Chicago: Museum of Contemporary Art.

Hall, Douglas. "Finley/Fine Collaboration," *Collaborations*. Exhibition catalogue. Cambridge, England: Kettle's Yard Gallery.

Hobbs, Robert Carleton. *Cornell Then, Sculpture Now*. Exhibition catalogue. New York: Sculpture Now, Inc. Gallery and Cornell University.

Kirshner, Judith Russi. *Words at Liberty*. Exhibition catalogue. Chicago: Museum of Contemporary Art.

Seldis, Henry and William Wilson. "Art Walk/A Critical Guide to the Galleries." *Los Angeles Times*, April 8, Part IV, 8.

1978

Frackman, Noel. "Arts Reviews." *Arts Magazine* (June): 36.

___________. "New York Reviews-Ronald Feldman." *Art News* (October): 176.

King, Pamela S. "Gallery Roundups: West Side Art Finally Takes a Trip Downtown." *Los Angeles Herald Examiner*, October 22, Section F, page F.

Kubiak, Richard. *Three Sculptors*. Exhibition catalogue. Santa Barbara, California: Santa Barbara Museum of Art.

Muchnic, Suzanne. "Art Review: Sculptures at Civic Center Mall." *Los Angeles Times*, October 23, Part IV, 10.

1979

Clisby, Roger D. *Aspects of Abstract: Recent West Coast Abstract Painting and Sculpture*. Exhibition catalogue. Sacramento, California: Crocker Art Museum.

Klausner, Betty. *California Hybrids*. Exhibition catalogue. New York: Alex Rosenberg Gallery.

Mallinson, Constance. "Metaphorical Landscapes." *Artweek*, June 2, 3.

Muchnic, Suzanne. "A Museum on a Campus Mall." *Los Angeles Times*, April 30.

Noah, Barbara. "Jud Fine at Margo Leavin." *Art in America* (Summer): 121.

Solomon, Poppy. *10 Sculptors/15 Works*. Exhibition catalogue. San Bernardino, California: Art Galleries, California State College, San Bernardino.

Wilson, William. "Art Walk/A Critical Guide to Galleries." *Los Angeles Times*, May 18, Part IV, 6.

1980

Armstrong, Richard. *Sculpture in California, 1975-1980*. Exhibition catalogue. San Diego, California: San Diego Museum of Art.

Wortz, Melinda. "Measurements of Time and Structures for Experience." *Artweek*, November 1, 5.

1981

Ball, Maudette. *Southern California Artists: 1940-1980*. Exhibition catalogue. Laguna Beach, California: Laguna Art Museum.

Cvikota, Thomas. *Possibly Overlooked Publications*. Chicago: Landfall Gallery.

Fine, Jud. "Polynesian/Polyhedron." *L.A.I.C.A. Journal* (Winter): 44-45.

Garver, Thomas H. *Downtown Los Angeles*. Exhibition catalogue. Madison, Wisconsin: Madison Art Center.

Hugo, Joan. "Jud Fine's Visual Paradigms." *Artweek*, November 28, 1.

Zeitlin, Marilyn. *Messages, Words and Images*. Exhibition catalogue. Reading, Pennsylvania: Freedman Gallery, Albright College.

1982

Hulten, Pontus, Suzanne Page and Ryszard Stanislawski. *Exchange Between Artists: An Experience for Museums*. Exhibition catalogue. Paris, France: Musée d'Art Moderne de la Ville de Paris.

Levine, Melinda. *Sculpture, '82*. Exhibition catalogue. Sonoma, California: University Art Gallery, Sonoma State University.

Or-Cahall, Christina, et al. *100 Years of California Sculpture*. Exhibition catalogue. Oakland, California: Oakland Museum of Art.

Smith, Michael. *Sculpture Sacramento*. Exhibition catalogue. Sacramento, California: City of Sacramento and Sacramento Metropolitan Arts Commission.

1983

Edgerton, Anne and Maurice Tuchman. "Modern and Contemporary Art Council, Young Talent Awards, 1963-1983." *Los Angeles County Museum of Art Bulletin*, 27-30.

__________. *Then and Now—Two Decades of Young Talent*. Exhibition catalogue. Los Angeles: Los Angeles County Museum of Art.

1984

Butterfield, Jan and Melinda Wortz. *California Sculpture Show*. Exhibition catalogue. Los Angeles: Fisher Gallery, University of Southern California.

Del Gado, Michael. "Pick of the Week." *L.A. Weekly*, May 11, 122.

1985

Fine, Jud and Michael H. Smith, eds. "A Conversation between Jud Fine, Frances Colpitt and Michael H. Smith," *Jud Fine, February 1985*. Exhibition catalogue. Los Angeles: Los Angeles Municipal Art Gallery.

Pincus, Robert. "Artist Sets Sail in a Sea of Telephone Poles," *San Diego Union*, September 15, E-2.

__________. "Fine's Installation Navigates New Sculptural Horizons," *San Diego Union*, September 15, E-2.

__________. "Vision, Concept and Object: The Art of Jud Fine, 1970-1985," *Jud Fine, February 1985*. Exhibition catalogue. Los Angeles: Los Angeles Municipal Art Gallery.

1987

McDonald, Robert. "Lines in Space." *Artweek*, February 28, 6.

1988

Onorato, Ronald J. *Jud Fine*. Exhibition catalogue. La Jolla, California: La Jolla Museum of Contemporary Art.

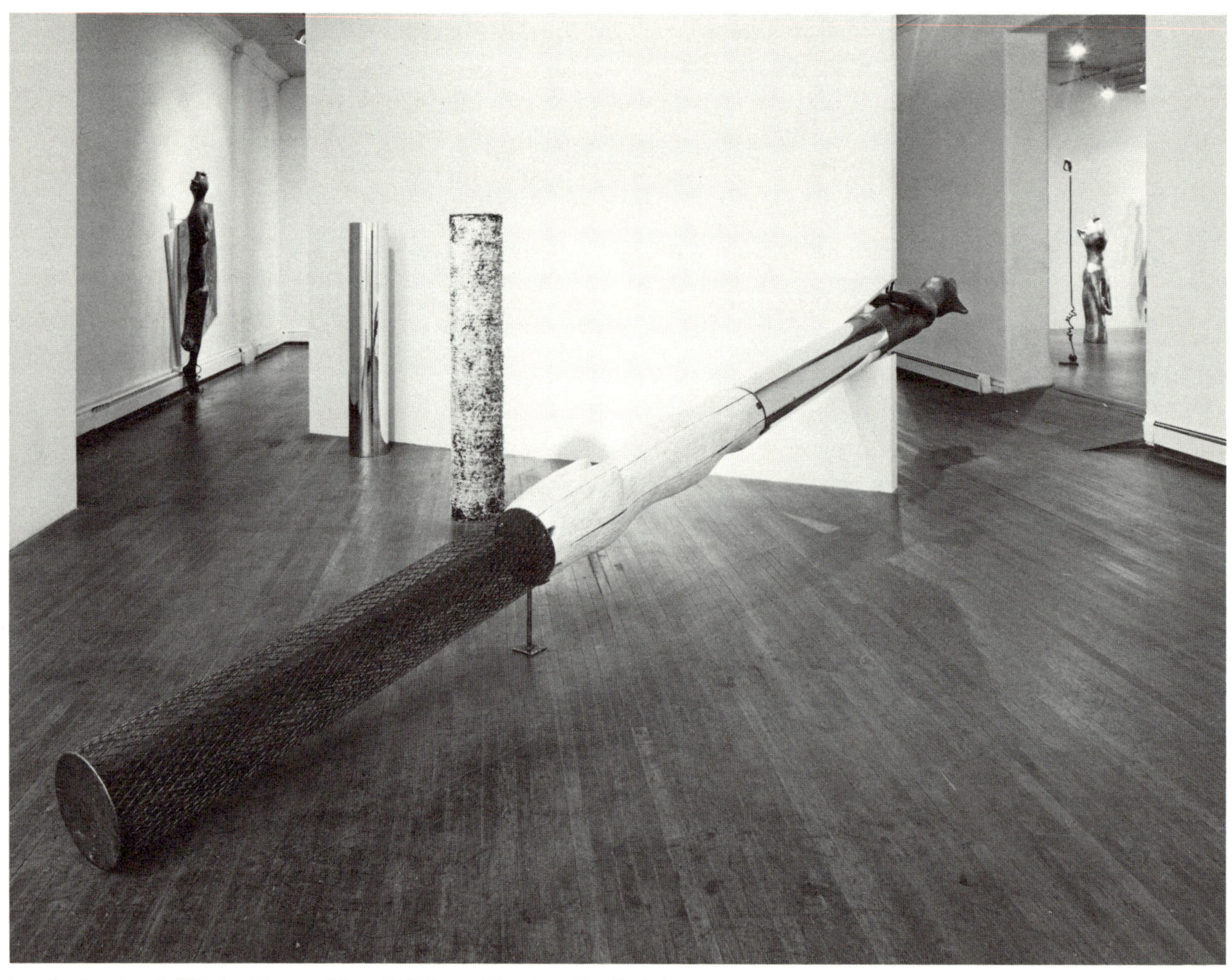

Installation detail, *“Divine Hunger,”* Ronald Feldman Fine Arts, New York City, 1987. Showing ***Long Pig II*** (foreground) and ***Dismembered (L.P.)***.

Fellows of Contemporary Art

The concept of the Fellows of Contemporary Art as developed by its founding members is unique. We are an independent organization established in 1975. Monies received from dues are used to underwrite our exhibitions and catalogs at tax-exempt educational institutions active in the field of contemporary art. We do not give grants, sponsor fundraising events, maintain a permanent facility or a permanent collection. In addition to the exhibition schedule, the Fellows have an active membership education program.

1976

Ed Moses Drawings 1958–1976
Frederick S. Wight Art Gallery
University of California, Los Angeles
Los Angeles, California
July 13–August 15, 1976
Catalog with essay by Joseph Masheck

1977

Unstretched Surfaces/Surfaces Libres
Los Angeles Institute of Contemporary Art
Los Angeles, California
November 5–December 16, 1977
Catalog with essays by Jean-Luc Bordeaux, Alfred Pacquement, and Pontus Hulten
Artists:
Bernadette Bour
Jerrold Burchman
Thierry Delaroyere
Daniel Dezeuze
Charles Christopher Hill
Christian Jaccard
Allan McCollum
Jean-Michel Meurice
Jean-Pierre Pincemin
Peter Plagens
Tom Wudl
Richard Yokomi

1978–80

Wallace Berman Retrospective
Otis Art Institute Gallery
Los Angeles, California
October 24–November 25, 1978
Catalog with essays by Robert Duncan and David Meltzer
Supported by a grant from the National Endowment for the Arts, Washington, D.C., a federal agency.
Exhibition traveled to: Fort Worth Art Museum, Fort Worth, Texas; University Art Museum, University of California, Berkeley, Berkeley, California; Seattle Art Museum, Seattle, Washington.

1979–80

Vija Celmins, A Survey Exhibition
Newport Harbor Art Museum
Newport Beach, California
December 15, 1979–February 3, 1980
Catalog with essay by Susan C. Larsen
Supported by a grant from the National Endowment for the Arts, Washington, D.C., a federal agency.
Exhibition traveled to: The Arts Club of Chicago, Chicago, Illinois; The Hudson River Museum, Yonkers, New York; The Corcoran Gallery of Art, Washington, D.C.

1980

Variations: Five Los Angeles Painters
University Art Galleries
University of Southern California
Los Angeles, California
October 20–November 23, 1980
Catalog with essay by Susan C. Larsen
Artists:
Robert Ackerman
Ed Gilliam
George Rodart
Don Suggs
Norton Wisdom

1981–82

Craig Kauffman Comprehensive Survey 1957–1980
La Jolla Museum of Contemporary Art
La Jolla, California
March 14–May 3, 1981
Catalog with essay by Robert McDonald
Supported by a grant from the National Endowment for the Arts, Washington, D.C., a federal agency.
Exhibition traveled to: Elvehjem Museum of Art, University of Wisconsin, Madison, Wisconsin; Anderson Gallery, Virginia Commonwealth University, Richmond, Virginia; The Oakland Museum, Oakland, California.

1981–82

Paul Wonner: Abstract Realist
San Francisco Museum of Modern Art
San Francisco, California
October 1–November 22, 1981
Catalog with essay by George W. Neubert
Exhibition traveled to: Marion Koogler McNay Art Institute, San Antonio, Texas; Los Angeles Municipal Art Gallery, Los Angeles, California.

1982–83

Changing Trends: Content and Style Twelve Southern California Painters
Laguna Beach Museum of Art
Laguna Beach, California
November 18, 1982–January 3, 1983
Catalog with essays by Francis Colpitt, Christopher Knight, Peter Plagens, and Robert Smith. Exhibition traveled to: Los Angeles Institute of Contemporary Art, Los Angeles, California.
Artists:
Robert Ackerman
Caron Colvin
Scott Grieger
Marvin Harden
James Hayward
Ron Linden
John Miller
Pierre Picot
George Rodart
Don Suggs
David Trowbridge
Tom Wudl

1983

Variations II: Seven Los Angeles Painters
Gallery at the Plaza
Security Pacific National Bank
Los Angeles, California
May 8–June 30, 1983
Catalog with essay by Constance Mallinson
Artists:
Roy Dowell
Kim Hubbard
David Lawson
William Mahan
Janet McCloud
Richard Sedivy
Hye Sook

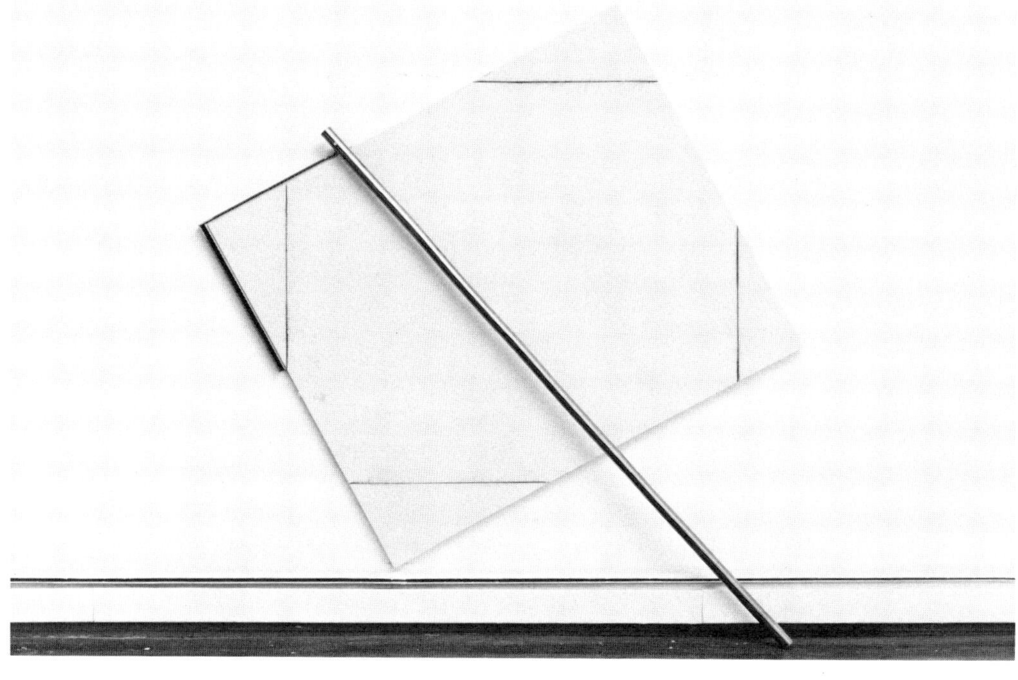

1984

Martha Alf Retrospective
Los Angeles Municipal Art Gallery
Los Angeles, California
March 6–April 1, 1984
Catalog with essay by Suzanne
Muchnic
Exhibition traveled to: San Francisco Art Institute, San Francisco,
California

1985

Sunshine and Shadow: Recent Painting in Southern California
Fisher Gallery
University of Southern California
Los Angeles, California
January 15–February 23, 1985
Catalog with essay by Susan C.
Larsen
Artists:

Robert Ackerman	Charles Christopher Hill
Richard Baker	Craig Kauffman
William Brice	Gary Lang
Karen Carson	Dan McCleary
Lois Colette	Arnold Mesches
Ronald Davis	John M. Miller
Richard Diebenkorn	Ed Moses
John Eden	Margit Omar
Llyn Foulkes	Marc Pally
Charles Garabedian	Pierre Picot
Candice Gawne	Peter Plagens
Joe Goode	Luis Serrano
James Hayward	Reesey Shaw
Roger Herman	Ernest Silva
	Tom Wudl

1985

James Turrell
The Museum of Contemporary Art
Los Angeles, California
November 13, 1985–February 9,
1986
A book entitled *Occluded Front
James Turrell* was published in conjunction with the exhibition.

1986

William Brice
The Museum of Contemporary Art
Los Angeles, California
September 1–October 19, 1986
Full color catalog with essay by
Richard Armstrong
Exhibition traveled to: Grey Art
Gallery and Study Center, New York
University, New York, New York

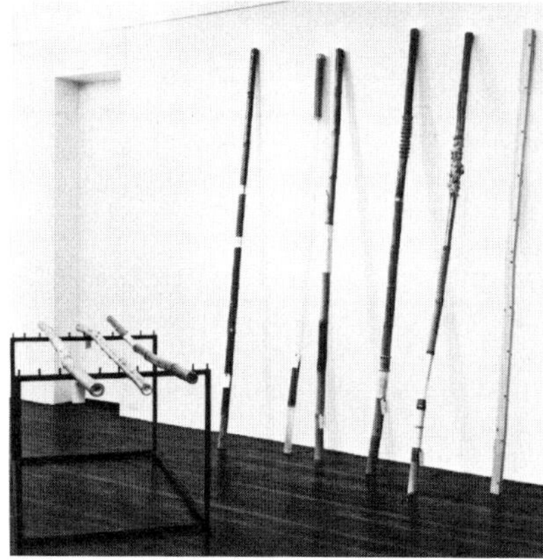

1987

*Variations III: Emerging Artists in
Southern California*
Los Angeles Contemporary
Exhibitions
Los Angeles, California
April 22–May 31, 1987
Catalog with essay by Melinda
Wortz
Exhibition traveled to: University of
California, Irvine, Fine Arts Gallery,
Irvine, California, and California
State University, Northridge, Art
Gallery, Northridge, California.
Artists:

Alvaro Asturias/ John Castagna	Julie Medwedeff
	Ihnsoon Nam
	Ed Nunnery
Hildegarde Duane/David Lamelas	Patti Podesta
	Deborah Small
	Rena Small
Tom Knechtel	Linda Ann Stark
Joyce Lightbody	

1987

Perpetual Motion
Santa Barbara Museum of Art
Santa Barbara, California
November 17, 1987–January 24,
1988
Catalog with essay by Betty
Turnbull
Artists:

Karen Carson	John Rogers
Margaret Nielsen	Tom Wudl

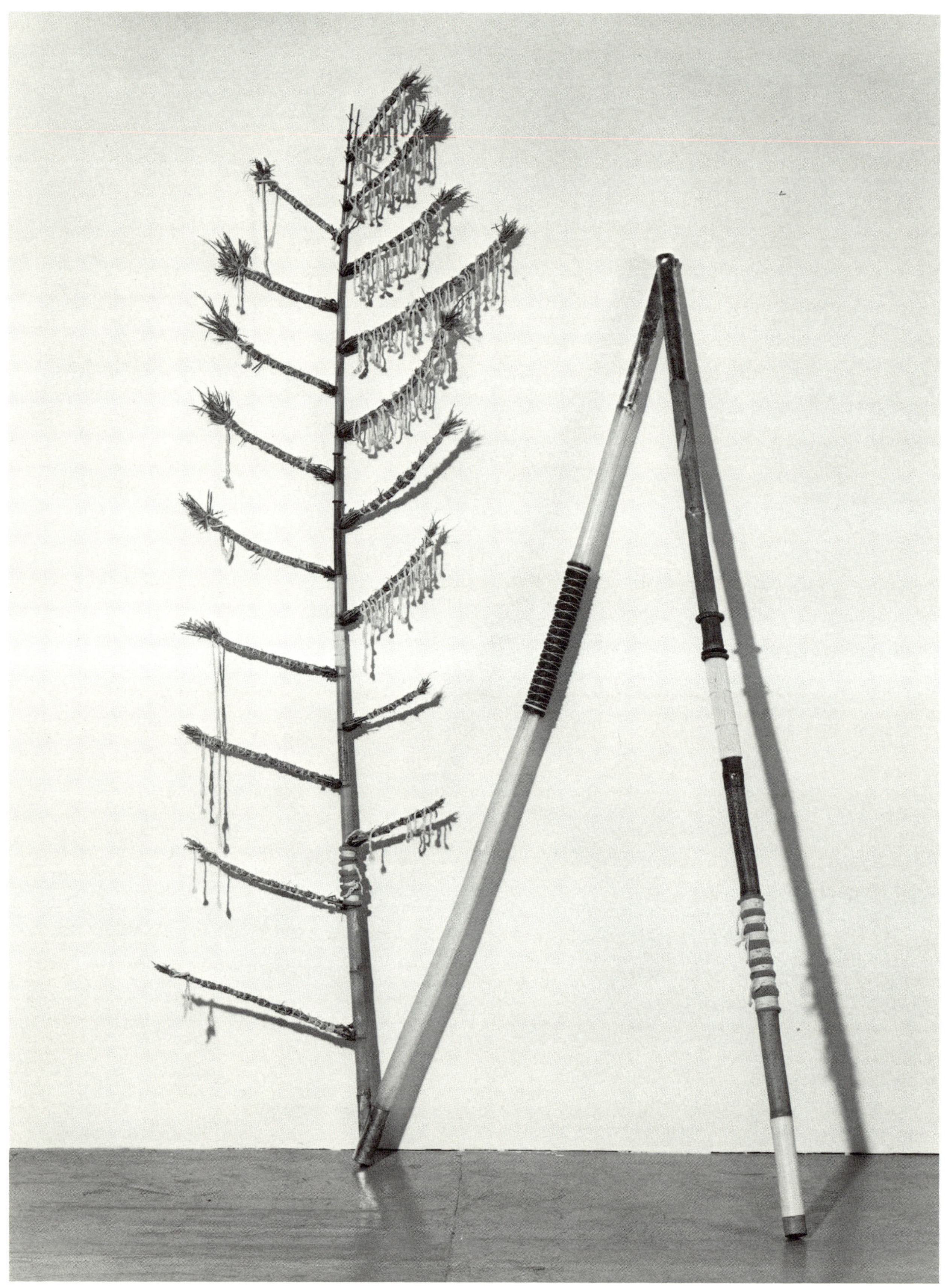

Acknowledgments

Without the generosity of lenders, no exhibition would be realized and we are grateful to the following for their cooperation: the Los Angeles County Museum of Art; the Museum of Contemporary Art, Chicago; the Museum of Contemporary Art, Los Angeles; the Santa Barbara Museum of Art; The Art Institute of Chicago; the Yale University Art Gallery; the Federal Reserve Bank of San Francisco; The Capital Group, Inc.; Ronald Feldman Fine Arts, New York City; Steven and Sue Antebi; Robert and Maryse Boxer; Susan and Bill Ehrlich; Marshall and Patricia Geller; Charles Hack; Margo H. Leavin; and Riko Mizuno. Robert McDonald, Director of the de Saisset Museum, has shown his commitment to Jud Fine and his work by sharing the exhibition with us. Many others have contributed in myriad ways to this endeavor. I was assisted and advised by the constant support of Charles Cochrane and Murray Gribin, who as members of the Fellows of Contemporary Art were intimately involved with the exhibition. Ronald Feldman, Margo Leavin, and Robert Murray willingly located works and have enthusiastically provided information and insights. In addition to members of the Museum staff, I was assisted by the thoughtful catalogue design of David Alcorn, by the editorial skills of Julie Dunn and Hugh Davies, Lynda Forsha, Mary Johnson, Anne Farrell, Diane Maxwell, Marie Vickers Horne, and Jane Carey. I appreciate the help and encouragement of Tom Flowers, David Jurist, and William Bulkley in installing the exhibition.

The entire project was really a collaboration between myself and two others: the artist, who was extremely generous with his time and efforts over the past two years enduring studio visits, interviews and innumerable phone calls, and my colleague Madeleine Grynsztejn, who has worked with me for the past year on **Jud Fine** and who, in addition to her perceptively written entries, has added immeasurably to the sense of clarity of both the exhibition and this publication. The entire project is the result of this enthusiastic three-way cooperative venture.

Ronald J. Onorato
Senior Curator

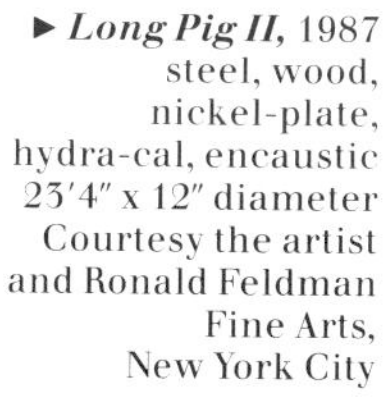

▶ *Long Pig II,* 1987
steel, wood,
nickel-plate,
hydra-cal, encaustic
23′4″ x 12″ diameter
Courtesy the artist
and Ronald Feldman
Fine Arts,
New York City

◀ *Watt's Irrevocable
Decision,* 1974
bamboo, fiberglass,
gold leaf, steel wool,
tape, string, lead,
ink, plastic, foam
rubber
9′1″ x 5′4″ x 30″
Collection Murray
and Ruth Gribin

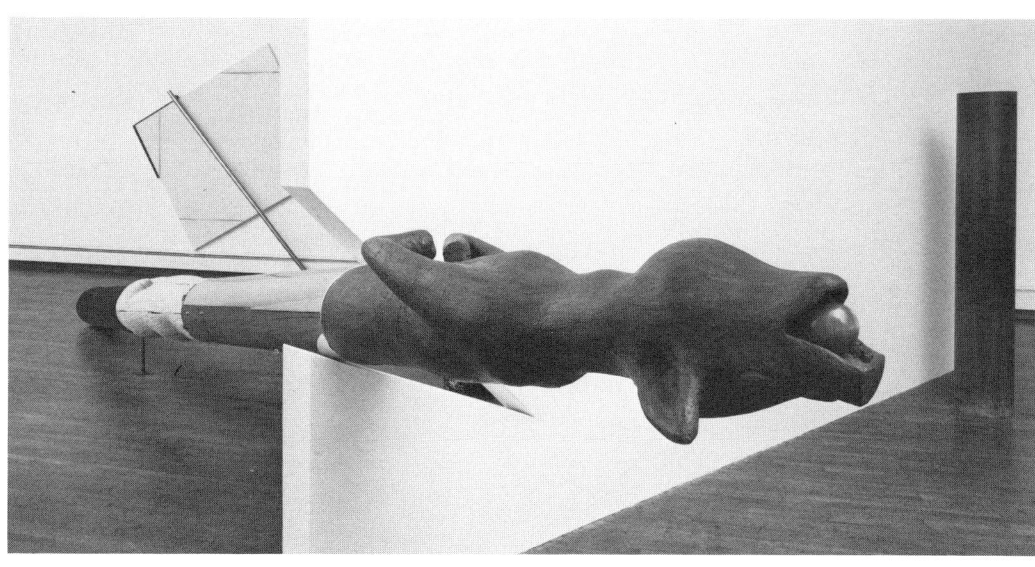

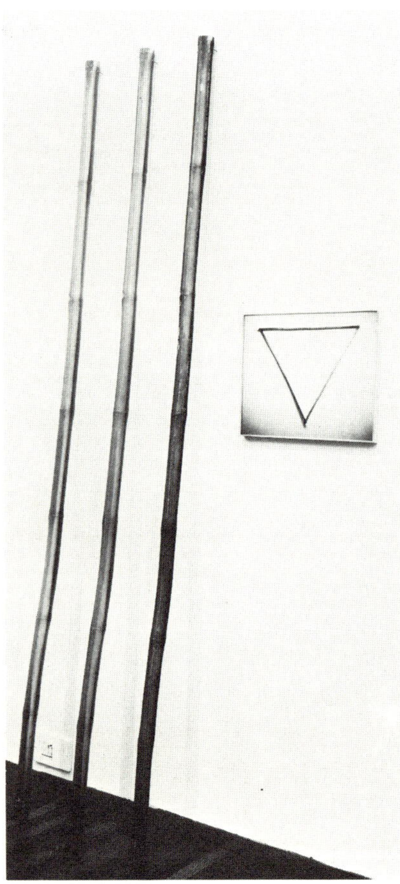

Primo Terce, 1973
fiberglass,
photograph
photograph 18″ x 18″,
poles 8′9″ x 2″
diameter
Courtesy Ronald
Feldman Fine Arts,
New York City

Design:
  Alcorn Visual
  Communications
Typography:
  Central Graphics
Printing: Rush Press
Editor: Julie Dunn
Photography:
D. James Dee:
  11,17,19,28,
  29,42,44,47
Eeva-Inkeri
  Photographers:
  11,20,26
Jud Fine:
  5,6,8,9,10,12,23
Robbert Flick: 38
Mary Kristen: 14
Los Angeles County
  Museum of Art:
  Title page
Douglas M. Parker:
  Cover,2,13,18,25,
  30,31,32,46,48
John Sturgeon: 34
The Art Institute of
  Chicago: 44
Kim Yasuda: 3,13